Modern Critical Interpretations
Ben Jonson's
Volpone, or the Fox

Modern Critical Interpretations

These and other titles in preparation

Modern Critical Interpretations

Ben Jonson's
Volpone, or the Fox

Edited and with an introduction by

Harold Bloom
Sterling Professor of the Humanities
Yale University

Chelsea House Publishers ◇ *1988*
NEW YORK ◇ NEW HAVEN ◇ PHILADELPHIA

© 1988 by Chelsea House Publishers, a division
of Chelsea House Educational Communications, Inc.
  345 Whitney Avenue, New Haven, CT 06511
  95 Madison Avenue, New York, NY 10016
  5068B West Chester Pike, Edgemont, PA 19028

Introduction © 1988 by Harold Bloom

Printed and bound in the United States of America

10 9 8 7 6 5 4 3 2 1

∞ The paper used in this publication meets the minimum
requirements of the American National Standard for
Permanence of Paper for Printed Library Materials,
Z39.48-1984.

Library of Congress Cataloging-in-Publication Data
Ben Jonson's Volpone, or the fox/edited with an introduction
by Harold Bloom.
    p. cm.—(Modern critical interpretations)
    Bibliography: p.
    Includes index.
    Contents: Volpone / William Empson—The false ending in
Volpone / Stephen Greenblatt—Comic form in Ben Jonson/
Leo Salingar—Comic language in Volpone [etc]
    ISBN 0–87754–914–1 (alk. paper): $24.50
    I. Jonson, Ben, 1573?–1637. Volpone.   [1. Jonson,
Ben, 1573?–1637. Volpone. 2. English literature—History and
criticism.]   I. Bloom, Harold.   II. Series.
PR2622.B46   1988   822'.3—dc19   87-15486

Contents

Editor's Note

This book gathers together a representative selection of the best modern critical interpretations of Ben Jonson's comedy, *Volpone, or the Fox*. The critical essays are reprinted here in the chronological order of their original publication. I am grateful to Cornelia Pearsall for her erudition and judgment in helping me to edit this volume.

My introduction first considers Jonson's critical stance, and then turns to *Volpone* as an example of how that classical moral and aesthetic position seems partly at variance with the villainous exuberance of the play. The late William Empson, perhaps the most gifted modern critic to come out of England, begins the chronological sequence of criticism with a corrective overview of *Volpone*, one that sees it as a farce that ends like a farce "though it had become so gripping."

In Stephen Greenblatt's study, the formal device of the false ending, at the close of act 4, is analyzed as a means for better understanding the very different end of act 5. Leo Salingar traces an overt metaphor for Jonson's comic form in the philosopher's stone of alchemy, instrumental both in *Volpone* and in Jonson's other comic masterpiece, *The Alchemist*. Comic language, rather than form, is L. A. Beaurline's subject in an essay that centers upon the extraordinary verbal energy of both Volpone and Mosca.

C. N. Manlove argues that the moral and exuberant elements in *Volpone* are increasingly in conflict during the play, and so are not combined to have a unitary dramatic effect. In Anne Barton's overview, *Volpone* is a play regenerated by *Sejanus* and complexly revisionary of it. Conspiracies and their interplay in *Volpone* are analyzed by William W. E. Slights, who concludes our volume by contextualizing Jonson's comedy in its "moment of acute political crisis in Jacobean England, immediately following the discovery of the Gunpowder Plot."

Introduction

In his conversations with (or harangues at) the Spenserian poet Drummond of Hawthornden in 1619, Ben Jonson repeated a joke of Sir Francis Bacon's:

> At his hither coming, Sir Francis Bacon said to him, He loved not to see poesy go on other feet than poetical dactyls and spondees.

Jonson, burly Laureate, portly Master Poet, rather grandly had marched into Scotland on foot, and greatly appreciated the Baconian compliment that poesy and Ben were identical. If Bacon presumably preferred Jonson, The Ancient, over Shakespeare, the Modern, this extraordinary evaluation was as remarkably reciprocated when Jonson gave Bacon the accolade as essayist and wisdom writer over Montaigne:

> One, though he be excellent and the chief, is not to be imitated alone; for never no imitator ever grew up to his author; likeness is always on this side truth. Yet there happened in my time one noble speaker who was full of gravity in his speaking; his language, where he could spare or pass by a jest, was nobly censorious. No man ever spake more neatly, more presly, more weightily, or suffered less emptiness, less idleness, in what he uttered. No member of his speech but consisted of his own graces. His hearers could not cough, or look aside from him, without loss. He commanded where he spoke, and had his judges angry and pleased at his devotion. No man had their affections more in his power. The fear of every man that heard him was lest he should make an end.

The art of this generous overpraise is that it is an elegant, if perhaps too neat, cento of commonplaces from Seneca, common precursor of Bacon and Montaigne. Jonson would have expected us to juxtapose this passage of *Timber, or Discoveries* with another, in which Montaigne, Shakespeare of essayists, is somewhat warily deprecated:

> Such are all the essayists, even their master Montaigne. These, in all they write, confess still what books they have read last, and therein their own folly so much, that they bring it to the stake raw and undigested; not that the place did need it neither, but that they thought themselves furnished and would vent it.

That is vigorous, nasty, and about as effective against Montaigne as were Jonson's ambivalent remarks against Shakespeare. Bacon himself, Jonson's authority, more cunningly said that the word "essay" was "late but the thing is ancient," which is shrewdly translated by Charles Whitney as: "Montaigne, the so-called first essayist, isn't as original as everyone thinks; *my* essays in fact represent the authentic continuity with a long tradition of skeptical, probing inquiry." But to take sides with Montaigne and Shakespeare against Bacon and Jonson would be easy, vulgar, and therefore disgusting. Bacon and Jonson, both too subtle and dialectical for mere paraphrase, were fighting on the side neither of Ancients nor Moderns. Modernity, as we always insist upon forgetting, is an Alexandrian concept, formulated by our grand precursor, Aristarchus, in defense of the first great Modernist poet, Callimachus. Doubtless, we cannot call Sir Francis Bacon the Nietzsche of his age, but we might begin to think of Nietzsche as the Bacon shadowing the threshold of our own era. Bacon too is concerned for the use and abuse of history for life, though he means by "life" something like civil society, the state, the future prospects of a people. Nietzsche, heroic vitalist, urged us to think of the earth, hardly a Baconian injunction, though Bacon has his own version of the Nietzschean admonition: "Try to live as though it were morning." Bacon and Nietzsche share the same resolution: do not live, work, or think as though you were a latecomer.

The heirs of Spenser in the earlier seventeenth century suffered a most acute sense of imaginative belatedness, typified by the Kabbalistic Henry Reynolds at the opening of his *Mythomystes*:

> I have thought upon the times we live in, and am forced to affirm the world is decrepit, and, out of its age & doating estate, subject to all the imperfections that are inseparable from that wrack and maim of Nature.

That is to replace history by poetry, or to read history as a Spenserian romance. Aristotle had placed poetry between philosophy and history, a stationing that Sir Philip Sidney had modified, perhaps slyly, by his apothegm that poetry took place between the precept and the example, and so could fulfill moral purposes that neither philosophy nor history could hope to serve. Bacon, in contrast, judged poetry to be a mere imitation of history, made to no end except the giving of pleasure. Spenser and Bacon were antipodes of thought and feeling, and their visions of history were almost irreconcilable. Their heirs necessarily possessed almost nothing in common. Ben Jonson and his school were divided from the Spenserians by multiple considerations, reflecting cultural choices that intricately fused religion, politics, and aesthetics.

Angus Fletcher, our great contemporary Spenserian, observes that Spenser "subordinates the insights of cyclical and scientific history to the Christian revelation of a prophetic historicism," though Fletcher shrewdly adds that this kind of poetic prophecy is as Orphic as it is Christian. I would add to Fletcher that such Orphic historicism is anti-Baconian in consequences, rather than as policy. Another major contemporary Spenserian, the late and much missed Isabel G. MacCaffrey, caught the precise agon between Spenser and the involuntary latecomer Bacon with admirable economy: "Bacon was later to disparage poets for submitting 'the shows of things to the desires of the mind,' but as both Sidney and Spenser affirm, those desires themselves bear witness to the presence of a realm of being inadequately figured by the shows of things."

Bacon's polemic against the poets presumably resulted from his desperate ambition to substitute his own historicism for the Orphic prophecies of the great poets. He too was a prophet, perhaps the most optimistic of British prophets before the young John Milton, and is rightly named as a counter-apocalyptic by Achsah Guibbory: "Like many of his contemporaries, Bacon believes that he is living in the 'autumn of the world,' that the end of time is approaching. But his sense that the end is not far off leads to a vision of progress, not an obsession with decay."

Charles Whitney, seeking to define Bacon's concept of modernity, notes the revision by misquotation that Bacon carries out in his use of the prophet Jeremiah:

> Bacon's spectacular misquotation of Jeremiah in *The Advancement of Learning's* best-known pronouncement on tradition and innovation reveals the problematic relationship of his instauration to the religious models. (The misquotation is repeated in

the *De Dignitate et Augmentis Scientiarum* and in the essay "Of Innovations.") Failure to appreciate that complex relationship (or to note misreading) has led commentators, among them Harold Bloom and Renato Poggioli. to construe the passage either as a bellwether of Enlightenment faith in free reason (Bloom) or as a defense of traditionalism (Poggioli).

In criticizing the "extreme affection" of either "Antiquity" or "Novelty" in learned men, Bacon says:

> Antiquity envieth there should be new additions, and novelty cannot be content to add but it must deface: surely the advice of the prophet is the true direction in this matter, *State super vias antiquas, et videte quaenam sit via recta et bona et ambulate in eas.* Antiquity deserveth that reverence, that men should make a stand thereupon and discover what is the best way; but when the discovery is well taken, then to make progression. And to speak truly, *Antiquitas saeculi juventus mundi.* These times are the ancient times, when the world is ancient, and not those which we account ancient *ordine retrogrado,* by a computation backward from ourselves.

Bacon's apparently moderate view of tradition and innovation here—the reversal of ancient and modern times being a sentiment found in several earlier contemporaries—reflects the generally reconciliatory attitude about the past assumed in the *Advancement.* The present is "old," clearly, because there has been cumulative development, fruitful imitation, and emulation. Even so, it has become necessary for Bacon to distort Jeremiah considerably. The Vulgate renders him thus:

> State super vias, et videte
> Et interrogate de semitis antiquis quae sit via bona,
> Et ambulate in ea,
> Et invenietis refrigirium animabus vestris

> (Stand in the ways, and look, and ask for the old paths, where the good way is, and walk in it, and find rest for your soul.)

Whitney interprets Jeremiah as meaning that "the right way is the old way," but that is to misread the prophet more weakly than Bacon did.

Bacon's *Stand in the old ways, and see which is the straight and good path, and walk in that,* omits asking for the old paths, because Jeremiah himself appears to mean that the good way is only one of the old paths, and the prophet's crucial empasis is: "walk in it," which is the entire burden of normative Judaism. Bacon indeed is battling against contemporary cultural undervaluation, including the Spenserians, with their study of the nostalgias, and his polemical insistence is that the ancients were the true moderns, and the moderns the true ancients, since those who arrived later knew more, and Bacon himself knew most of all.

II

The contemporary critic-scholar Thomas M. Greene, who may be our very last Renaissance Humanist, battles his own profound sense of belatedness in a splendid essay on "Ben Jonson and the Centered Self":

> The equilibrated energy of the centered self is most amply demonstrated by Jonson's *Timber*. The stress in that work falls on the faculty of judgment, and in fact it demonstrates this faculty at work, choosing among authors and passages, discriminating conduct and style.
>
> > Opinion is a light, vain, crude, and imperfect thing, settled in the imagination, but never arriving at the understanding, there to obtain the tincture of reason.
>
> The passages gathered in *Timber* are exercises of the reasonable understanding. A sentence like the one quoted seems to place the imagination in an outer layer of consciousness, where the centrifugal "opinion" can momentarily alight. The understanding is further within, at the psychic center of gravity, impervious to the flights of the butterfly-caprice. All of *Timber*, whether or not "original" in the vulgar sense, seems to issue from this center of gravity.

Greene, a well-tempered Humanist, powerful and crafty, but in the last ditch, centers upon *Timber* as a gathering of "exercises of the reasonable understanding." Thirty years ago, the great Humanist William K. Wimsatt, Jr., Greene's mentor as well as mine, asserted rather more for *Timber*:

> Jonson's stout and craftsmanly common sense about imitation, shown even more convincingly in his practice than in his precepts, may be taken as the key to a theory of poetry which

stressed hard work—imitation, practice, study, art (and with these but one poor pennyworth of *ingenium*)—a theory too which stressed poems squared off by the norm of reality. This theory celebrated the mobility and power of poetry, but it included no hymn to spontaneity or to what today we think of as the creative imagination. It included no statement even remotely parallel to that of Sidney about the free range of wit within its zodiac or that of Bacon about poetry submitting the shows of reality to the desires of the mind. Some deviation or wavering from the classic norm may appear in Jonson's treatment of such a minor article as that prescribing the unity of place—and we have seen that he is guilty of defying the authority of the antique critics. But he is the first English man of letters to exhibit a nearly complete and consistent neo-classicism. His historical importance is that he throws out a vigorous announcement of the rule from which in the next generation Dryden is to be engaged in politely rationalized recessions. One basic problem which Jonson leaves us pondering (the same as that posed implicitly once before, by a strong appreciator of poetic inspiration, Longinus) might be formulated as follows: Does an aesthetic norm of objective reality entail a *genetic* theory of conscious and strenuous artistic effort? If a poet is to give us a truthful account of general human nature, does this poet have to be a learned consumer of midnight oil, a graduate in grammar, logic, and rhetoric, and in the higher liberal disciplines? Or on the other hand: Does an aesthetic norm of personal expression entail a genetic theory of untrammeled and unstudied inspiration? If a poet is to tell the truth as he himself most really and deeply experiences it, does he have to be a rebel against tradition and conventional education, a Bohemian, long-haired, and unwashed, a defiler of ancestral ashes?

On this view, Jonson is more on the side of Ancients against Moderns than his master Bacon was, and that must be right. But how could Jonson have inaugurated English neoclassicism, when he seems to have held a Stoic or cyclical theory of history? His identification with Horace, I suspect, was not truly founded upon some supposed and rather dubious parallel between Roman and English history, despite the persuasive arguments of Achsah Guibbory in *The Map of Time*. Whatever Horace's actual temperament may have been, we know that the fierce and violent Jonson, burly Ben indeed, was not exactly a natural Stoic. Can we not surmise that Jonson's preference for the Ancients was antithetical, against the grain, a correction of the most vehement sensibility ever possessed by a major English poet? History, including the events of his own time, disgusted the passionate moralist Jonson, who turned to Stoicism and the Ancients so as to withdraw from what might have provoked him to a madness of no use to literature.

There is a great passage in *Timber* in praise of Bacon, "the late Lord Saint Albans," that can serve to sum up both of these great minds on the virtues of the Ancients, and on the possibility of becoming an Ancient in your own time:

> It was well noted by the late Lord Saint Albans, that the study of words is the first distemper of learning; vain matter the second; and third distemper is deceit, or the likeness of truth, imposture held up by credulity. All these are the cobwebs of learning, and to let them grow in us is either sluttish or foolish. Nothing is more ridiculous than to make an author a dictator, as the schools have done Aristotle. The damage is infinite knowledge receives by it; for to many things a man should owe but a temporary belief, and a suspension of his own judgment, not an absolute resignation of himself, or a perpetual captivity. Let Aristotle and others have their dues; but if we can make farther discoveries of truth and fitness than they, why are we envied? Let us beware, while we strive to add, we do not diminish or deface; we may improve, but not augment. By discrediting falsehood, truth grows in request. We must not go about, like men anguished and perplexed for vicious affectation of praise, but calmly study the separation of opinions, find the errors have intervened, awake antiquity, call former times into question; but make no parties with the present, nor follow any fierce undertakers, mingle no matter of doubtful credit with the simplicity of truth; but gently stir the mould about the root of the question, and avoid all digladiations, facility of credit, or superstitious simplicity, seek the consonancy and concatenation of truth; stoop only to point of necessity, and what leads to convenience. Then make exact animadversion where style hath degenerated, where flourished and thrived in choiceness of phrase, round and clean composition of sentence, sweet falling of the clause, varying an illustration by tropes and figures, weight of matter, worth of subject, soundness of argument, life of invention, and depth of

judgment. This is *monte potiri,* to get the hill; for no perfect discovery can be made upon a flat or a level.

To discover the errors that have intervened is to awaken antiquity while making no alliances with the present, yet also is to call all former times into question. Here, at least, Jonson admirably joins himself to Bacon, and prepares the way for Milton's much more drastic transumption of the tradition.

III

Jonson's magnificent vehemence carries him over to Volpone's side, in defiance of Jonsonian moral theory. Not that Volpone (and the plebeian Mosca even more so) is not hideously punished. He—like Mosca—is outrageously overpunished, which may be Jonson's self-punishment for the imaginative introjection of his greatest creation. Perhaps Jonson is chastising us also, knowing that we too would delight in Volpone. The representation of gusto, when worked with Jonson's power, becomes a gusto that captivates us, so that it scarcely matters if we remember how wicked Volpone is supposed to be. Massively aware of this paradox, distrusting the theatrical while creating Volpone as a genius of theatricality, Jonson takes moral revenge upon Volpone, the audience, and even himself. The imagination wishes to be indulged, and delights in being deceived. No playgoer or reader wishes to see Volpone's deceptions fail, and our delight is surely Jonson's delight also.

Robert M. Adams has some shrewd comments upon what I suppose we might want to call Jonson's ambivalences towards the theater:

> The tone of punishment and correction runs through a lot of Jonson's dramatic work; there are passages which don't come far short of suggesting that he thought the work itself a form of correction, if not punishment, for the audience: "physic of the mind" was one of his terms.

Jonson might have observed that he was following Aristotle's precepts, yet a "physic of the mind" does seem stronger than a catharsis. You tend to receive worse than you (badly) merit in Jonson, and that hardly purges you of fear. It is something of a mystery anyway why Jonson believed Volpone and Mosca needed to be so severely punished. Except for his exasperated attempt to rape Celia, Volpone preys only upon those who deserve to be fleeced, and thus defrauds only the fraudulent. Nor does

Jonson represent Volpone's failed lust for Celia as being without its own imaginative opulence. As with Sir Epicure Mammon in *The Alchemist,* we hear in Volpone's mad eloquence the equivocal splendor of a depraved will corrupting imagination to its own purposes:

> CELIA: Some sérene blast me, or dire lightning strike
>   This my offending face!
> VOLPONE: Why droops my Celia?
>   Thou hast, in place of a base husband, found
>   A worthy lover: use thy fortune well,
>   With secrecy and pleasure. See, behold,
>   What thou art queen of; not in expectation,
>   As I feed others: but possessed and crowned.
>   See here a rope of pearl; and each, more orient
>   Than that the brave Egyptian queen caroused:
>   Dissolve and drink them. See, a carbuncle
>   May put out both the eyes of our St. Mark;
>   A diamond, would have bought Lollia Paulina,
>   When she came in like star-light, hid with jewels,
>   That were the spoils of provinces; take these,
>   And wear, and lose them: yet remains an earring
>   To purchase them again, and this whole state.
>   A gem but worth a private patrimony,
>   Is nothing: we will eat such at a meal.
>   The heads of parrots, tongues of nightingales,
>   The brains of peacocks, and of ostriches,
>   Shall be our food: and, could we get the phoenix,
>   Though nature lost her kind, she were our dish.
> CELIA: Good sir, these things might move a mind affected
>   With such delights; but I, whose innocence
>   Is all I can think wealthy, or worth th'enjoying,
>   And which, once lost, I have nought to lose beyond it,
>   Cannot be taken with these sensual baits:
>   If you have conscience—
> VOLPONE: 'Tis the beggar's virtue;
>   If thou hast wisdom, hear me, Celia.
>   Thy baths shall be the juice of gilly-flowers,
>   Spirit of roses, and of violets,
>   The milk of unicorns, and panthers' breath
>   Gathered in bags, and mixed with Cretan wines.

Our drink shall be prepared gold and amber;
Which we will take, until my roof whirl around
With the vertigo: and my dwarf shall dance,
My eunuch sing, my fool make up the antic,
Whilst we, in changèd shapes, act Ovid's tales,
Thou, like Europa now, and I like Jove,
Then I like Mars, and thou like Erycine:
So, of the rest, till we have quite run through,
And wearied all the fables of the gods.
Then will I have thee in more modern forms,
Attirèd like some sprightly dame of France,
Brave Tuscan lady, or proud Spanish beauty;
Sometimes, unto the Persian Sophy's wife,
Or the Grand Signor's mistress; and, for change,
To one of our most artful courtesans,
Or some quick Negro, or cold Russian;
And I will meet thee in as many shapes:
Where we may so transfuse our wandering souls
Out at our lips, and score up sums of pleasures.

It is difficult to believe that Jonson did not admire the superb audacity of Volpone's hyperboles, which out-Marlowe Marlowe. "Could we get the phoenix, / Though nature lost her kind, she were our dish," is particularly fine, as that firebird, mythical and immortal, is always present only in one incarnation at any single moment. Heroic in the bravura of his lust, the Ovidian Volpone charms us by the delicious zeal with which he envisions Celia's changes of costume. Sir Epicure Mammon holds on always in my memory for his energetic "here's the rich Peru," but Volpone is positively endearing as he gets carried away in transports of voluptuousness, and bursts into strains of Catullus in his exuberance:

Come, my Celia, let us prove,
While we can, the sports of love,
Time will not be ours for ever,
He, at length, our good will sever;
Spend not then his gifts in vain:
Suns that set may rise again;
But if once we lose this light,
'Tis with us perpetual night.
Why should we defer our joys?
Fame and rumor are but toys.

Cannot we delude the eyes
Of a few poor household spies?
Or his easier ears beguile,
Thus removéd by our wile?—
'Tis no sin love's fruits to steal;
But the sweet thefts to reveal,
To be taken, to be seen,
These have crimes accounted been.

Jonas Barish, moved by his depth of Jonsonian scholarship to a Jonsonian moralizing, reads Volpone's Ovidian and Catullan allusions as evidence that: "Folly, vanity, lust, have been, are, will be. At any given moment their practioners are legion, and often interchangeable." Yes, and doubtless Jonson would have been gratified, but what about the verve, wit, lyric force, and intoxicating eloquence with which Jonson has endowed Volpone? Foolish and vain lusters may be interchangable, but whom would you get if you gave up Volpone? We are again in the paradox of Jonson's theatrical art at its most extraordinary, which brings Volpone back to delight us after he has been so cruelly sentenced:

[VOLPONE comes forward.]
The seasoning of a play is the applause.
Now, though the fox be punished by the laws,
He yet doth hope, there is no suffering due,
For any fact which he hath done 'gainst you;
If there be, censure him; here he doubtful stands:
If not, fare jovially, and clap your hands. [Exit.]
THE END

Where can we find the Jonsonian ambivalence in this? Volpone indeed has done nothing except entertain us, richly beyond most rivals. Barish strongly remarks that when Jonson imposes a terrible punishment upon Volpone, we feel betrayed. I would use a darker word, and say that we are outraged, though we grant that Volpone is outrageous. Jonson's moral aesthetic was not quite what he thought it to be. His savage relish in Volpone's tricks is also a savage relish for the stage, and so also a savage appreciation for the savagery of his audience.

Volpone

William Empson

A good deal of standardization of opinion and critical method became
necessary when Eng. Lit. became a large profession, and I think the results
are often mistaken; but it is naturally hard to make my colleagues agree
with any such judgement. The best opportunity is where the credibility
gap appears at an unexpected place—where the university teachers or ex-
aminers feel slightly appalled at the apparently orthodox opinions which
the children (whose schoolteachers usually retain more hold upon their
loyalty and affection than any later teacher) write sturdily down. When I
first met Professor L. C. Knights, which was fairly recently at Gambier,
Ohio, there was some mention of the yearly examinations, and he said,
"The very saddest time of all." I said, "You mean you find the students
haven't followed what you told them?" "Well, of course, there is that too,"
he said, "but sometimes, you know, they have." This delicacy of feeling
proved at once that he was not a Leavisite in any harmful way. Thinking
it over, I doubt whether he had literally said these things which he did not
like to read in an answer; they would be deductions from his position, or
parodies of it, which he had not foreseen the need for a warning against. I
fancy that the salutary shock which he adumbrated here arises more frequently about Ben Jonson than about any other standard author. The argument has a more direct impact upon an English than an American
professional, because in England a large proportion of the students who
are being prepared to read Eng. Lit. at university have to pass examinations
in either *Volpone* or *The Alchemist* (to which the same troubles apply in a

From *The Hudson Review* 21, no. 4 (Winter 1968–69). © 1969 by *The Hudson Review*.

rather different way); but many of my American colleagues would feel the same shock if faced with the same documents.

What the children write down is a good deal hotter and cruder than most of the stuff in the textbooks, but it is the same grand muddle which appeared so novel and charming about half a century ago. They write: "Volpone is a miser. The play does nothing but denounce misers, and he is the worst one, because he worships his gold. All the characters are loathsome except the young couple, and they are subnormal because they talk in a conventional poetic style; but Volpone is the most loathsome, as he blasphemes. Jonson had a theory about plays, that they ought to make you sick of being wicked, and the reason why his plays are so good is that they make you so sick. They are written in poetry which is meant to excite contempt and nausea, and that is why it is such good poetry. Good people enjoy these plays very much, though they are in pain all the time, aching for the tortures to begin." It is extraordinary to me that a man can "mark" a large number of these answers straight on end and still believe what they say.

At first I thought I knew an immediate reply: that Volpone cannot be a miser, because he offers to lavish upon Celia his whole fortune—he is a "dashing" lover, which was an equally familiar type, and a quite different one. But my opponents had been properly indoctrinated, and would readily answer that this minor error in characterisation, necessary for the plot, was not risked till the "type" of Volpone had been established firmly. I made a point of asking whether the students who wrote and argued like this had ever seen a performance of "Punch and Judy," at the seaside perhaps, and they all said they had, though of course only long, long before. So it is not true that there had been any "failure of tradition," only that a false tradition, like a cuckoo's egg, had been imposed.

Jonson himself was prone to instruct his audiences, knowing that he had often been misunderstood, and *Volpone* as he planned it begins with a prologue telling the audience to laugh. Laughing is good for them, he says, and he is not attacking any individual sinners at the moment:

> All gall and copper as from his ink he draineth;
> Only a little salt remaineth.
> Wherewith he'll rub your cheeks till, red with laughter,
> They will look fresh a week after.

Physiological reactions vary with period and fashion a great deal more than we easily realise, and maybe some cheeks actually did go on looking red for several days after the explosions of laughter caused by seeing the famous farce. But, even granting that what the author announces is incredible, a man who chose to start off like this could not have intended what the modern students describe—a play of almost unbearable horror, regularly screwing itself up to points which are still more nearly unbearable. It seems plain to me that the pietistic strain in Eng. Lit., as it has developed during the last forty years or so, regularly produces crippled or perverted moral judgements, wholly out of contact with the basic tone of feeling of the older works which they purport to interpret; and I have to say this in a general or pompous way, because I find that when I make jokes intended to say it lightly they are regarded as merely in bad taste.

It was quite frequent on the sands, as I remember, for one of the kids to bellow because "Punch" was too hard to take, and this unfortunate would be carried away by its nurse; but the elder children, when I was one, proud that they could take it, would laugh on till the final hanging of Punch as their Victorian parents had done at the same age. I have been secretly afraid of the theatre ever since, but I feel I know what it is about. However, the harshness is not invariable; "rogue sentiment" does not have to be offset by this primitive bitter flavour. The first audiences of *The Winter's Tale* (and they were Jonson's public too) enjoyed seeing Autolycus pick pockets, and readily agreed that he was at bottom a good man, who would help the lovers and thus forward the plot; though in real life they would have got him hanged if they had caught him. You may decide that rogue sentiment is a rather silly self-indulgence, but that is no reason for blinding yourself to its frequent occurrence in plays.

After the prologue, the curtain opens on Volpone worshipping his gold, a handsome piece of rhetoric, intended of course to establish the main theme powerfully at once. I agree that the references, though classical rather than Christian, are meant to imply that worshipping gold is a bad thing; and at first the audience necessarily supposes that Volpone is being satirized, since he is the only character yet in view. But an actor, however much he has been lectured by symbolist critics, feels bound to treat the soliloquy as satire intended by the character. The mind of Volpone needs to be presented as powerful and rather sinister; to make him an earnest gold-worshipper would reduce him to a quirky eccentric. Mosca then starts flattering Volpone, and the audience must assume, while rapidly picking up the social situation, that these things are what Volpone likes to be told—it gives a slightly unusual, therefore less boring, kind of dramatic exposition. They hear at once that Volpone is morally much better than the other rich men in Venice, never hurting the poor at all, and is positively the opposite of a miser because his occupation and his delight is to cheat misers as they deserve. No wonder we found him mocking them when alone—Jonson expects the audience to reinterpret the "imagery" when it appreciates the "character." The presumption of our modern literary critics that no audience could jump this little fence amounts to presuming that all audiences are subhuman.

I do not mean to deny that the lead-in of the play is consistent with its whole plot and setting; indeed, the setting made the plot seem almost credible. London was jealous of Venice, as an aggressive leader of international maritime trade, because London wanted to do that on a bigger scale. "Terrible pigs, that tyrannous Council of Ten; they never think of anything but money"—Jonson could rely upon getting this reaction even from business men in his audience, while most of the audience were enjoying the play as a satire upon business men. Naturally, Volpone is tainted by the society which has produced him, and seems unable to imagine any directly good way of life—cheating the cheats is about all he can rise to. As the play develops, this comes to seem pathetic; but one cannot feel that the effect is intended, because the frame of mind of Jonson is so close to that of his hero. The story goes that he conceived this play (as a triumphant popular farce) and the *Masque of Blackness* (as delightful for the court) together in a debtors' prison, and felt confident that they would set him up, as they did. So far as he identifies himself with Volpone it is because of the enthusiasm of his own breakthrough into fortune, which he need not be supposed to regard morosely.

We next meet the three unappetizing deviants, dwarf, eunuch and hermaphrodite, whom Volpone keeps for his amusement or pleasure, and I can't deny that he seems here particularly short of ideas for gracious living. But as Velasquez was just then painting the similar figures who satisfied the Court of Spain it would be hard to argue that Jonson was malignantly making his satire worse than the reality. We are hampered in reading, here and later (e.g., the rhymes here about the previous incarnations of the hermaphrodite, and later the prose speech of Volpone as mountebank), by a fault which is regularly corrected in production; Johnson used to add words for the printer whenever he felt touchily proud of an effect which had failed on the stage, and these bits need taking out again. The audience would accept three hours from Shakespeare but only two and a half from Jonson, and he was in an uneasy relation, resentful though admiring, to his older and more experienced rival. Now, Shakespeare had been winning all hearts by the breadth of poetry of his clowns, and Jonson had never quite accepted them—nor would we, if we had to meet them. It is cheerful to imagine the immense decisiveness with which the present Elizabeth would silence her Royal Clown, if forced to have one. Still, the formula of Erasmus was well within the powers of sympathy of Jonson, and the final lyric of the scene here (Fools, they are the only nation) comes off very well. Nowadays many critics assume that the first audiences would regard the scene as an attack on the top-class habit of keeping a resident clown, and this, I do submit, is quite unhistorical. So far from that, the mountainous scholar would be simpering as he held the pose in his spangled tights; he would expect to be as much loved for it as Feste or Touchstone. How cross he would be if he heard our modern experts praise the scene because it excites so much disgust. We should maybe praise Jonson for bringing a bit of reality into the theme of the pet lunatic, but we cannot say that he meant it to stand out as satire; after all, no Elizabethan playwright except Shakespeare was good at writing the mad talk which they felt to be somehow needed.

The *Broken Compass* (1958) by E. B. Partridge is a book always on the university shelves which firmly encourages the delusions of the students. It is important to realise, I think, that his remarks about the "imagery" take for granted that you accept passively the words on the page, and never imagine yourself producing the play, telling the actors what to do:

> Mosca tells Corvino the dwarf the fool and the eunuch are only a few of Volpone's many bastards . . . may be talking loosely . . . so far as the imagery is concerned, whether he is telling the truth does not matter, because the connection between Volpone and his "family" is made in the listener's mind.

This presumes that the listener is imbecile, so much broken down by the loathsome theory of Imagism that he is unable to recognise even a farcically plain human situation. What you see on the stage, when Mosca tells this lie to Corvino, is Volpone wrestling not to betray his trick by exploding with laughter; Mosca has told it merely in order to tease him. At least, there is no other effective way to act the thing, but I recognise that a decisive moral judgement has to be made before the producer accepts the obvious here. A pietistic reader immediately gulps down the bit of scandal (though not because of "imagery"—that is only an excuse; *what* image?). But the type of spectator Jonson relied upon getting was eager for the horrible old miser to be deceived, and regarded his pious affectation of shock on hearing the scandal as further gross hypocrisy. This man was not tempted to believe the scandal, because for him it was not even part of the "atmosphere." Mallarmé and Verlaine, it seems fair to remember, did not employ their treasured Symbolism to insinuate scandal, as at a cats' teaparty; this bold application of the method was invented by our pious Establishment critics. But maybe the great anti-intellectual movement did rather deserve to be misused.

Volpone is an extremist or desperate character, I do not deny; that is why he is equipped to show us the commercial hell of Venice; but he is on our side against it, as the earlier literary guides through hell had always been. We are expected to feel a basic sympathy for him, as for Punch; and this is the chief source of the poetry of the play. Simple-minded readers, and I too, expect poetry to have a certain warmth and expansiveness, even a feeling of generosity, though this may perhaps be given merely by a process of generalisation, a sudden insight into life as a whole. The modern refusal to recognise this in Jonson is unfair to him. Towards the end of the first act, when the second horrible old miser totters away after being cheated, Volpone bounds from his sickbed and generalises about them:

> So many cares, so many maladies,
> So many fears attending on old age,
> Yea, death so often called

and yet they are still so eager to cheat for money that they have become absurdly easy to cheat. Volpone here is remarkably unlike what the students say; he is brooding like an archangel over the self-torturing folly of mankind. Mosca is evidently accustomed to sentiments like this, though he feels more at home when encouraging the sense of triumph:

VOLPONE: Despatch, despatch; I long to have possession
Of my new present.
MOSCA: That, and thousands more
I hope to see you lord of.
VOLPONE: Thanks, kind Mosca.
MOSCA: And that, when I am lost in blended dust,
And thousands such as I am, in succession—
VOLPONE: Nay that were too much Mosca—
MOSCA: You shall live
Still, to delude these harpies.
VOLPONE: Loving Mosca!
Tis well; my pillow now, and let him enter.

The golden glow of this poetry is rare in Jonson's plays, and depends here upon a moral sympathy, even if a mixed and fleeting one, from the audience to the comic hero. Mosca and Volpone are right, as well as clever and brave, to cheat the grandees of Venice. To become morally independent of one's formative society in this way is the grandest theme of all literature, because it is the only means of moral progress, the establishment of some higher ethical concept. Our modern neo-Christian critics seem to imply that what Jesus Christ did, let alone Robin Hood and Huckleberry Finn, is particularly contemptible to them; they assume that any established ortho- doxy must be supported. I suppose this movement was prophesied by Wyndham Lewis in *The Art of Being Ruled* (1926), which recommended for us (whatever he meant by it) a total subservience, ready to lick the boots of any policeman in power. No one would deny that to set oneself up as morally independent carries great dangers, even in minor cases, and a play on the topic needs to present them firmly. None the less, the very basis of operation of *Volpone* is the familiar sentiment about the highwayman or the bootlegger, which though it feels obvious to the whole audience is rather complex. Surely it is peculiar that these scholarly critics, who claim to be recovering for us the grand old tradition which we have lost, have less understanding of it than the first man they might ask in the street, and talk as if they were androids from Andromeda.

Going back to the incident of the hero in triumph, just quoted: the audience was sure to laugh because he is shown loving his male flatterer, who must give him a kiss before the words "Tis well." Volpone indeed hungers for the love of Mosca whenever he is triumphant, though he is also ready to enjoy the ladies, and lets drop in act 5 that Mosca is no use for sodomy. Italians were assumed to be highly sophisticated in such mat- ters, but the main story here did not seem foreign at all. The life of a successful criminal is miserable unless there is someone he can boast to while he drinks, telling his secrets, and he is bound to love this person because his social isolation does not allow him any other intimacy; and yet this person, by the mere logic of having excluded the rule of law, is com- mitted to betraying him. I never feel sure about the logic of this, and wicked gentry often dodged it, but it was accepted as common experience. Consider the Jew of Malta, who after losing his daughter buys a Turkish slave. He at once wins the heart of this earnest affectionate man by boasting of his crimes, and the slave betrays him to a Maltese prostitute merely because he cannot bear not to boast of his good luck in getting such a wonderfully wicked master. The betrayals of Volpone by Mosca, and of Mosca by Volpone, are I think more deeply felt and understood by the author, but he would regard them as interesting examples of this well-known and accepted moral.

The English visitors need not have much interpretation piled onto them; their chief effect, being ridiculous in a relaxed and fairly homely manner, is to lighten a play which would otherwise be too tense for a comedy. They do show the importance of Venice in the minds of Londoners; Sir Politic imagines himself to be a spy, and it is assumed that this is a recognized line of endeavour. Also, to a slight extent, the contact of these everyday figures with the fantastic Volpone, who is almost too much an antique Roman even to be a Venetian, helps to make him a contact-man for the audience too. This is not done by making him friends with Lady Would-be, but by making him laugh at her from the same side as the audience. Always a man of restless and powerful intelligence, he is I think the first character in English Literature who is bored by a literary critic. (Hamlet had already been shown as bored, but as a literary critic he is himself fairly boring.) When Lady Would-be threatens to cheer the sickbed of Volpone by a survey of the Italian poets, he is almost driven to betray his secret by leaping up and escaping, or so he tells Mosca afterwards to express the violence of his boredom. Mr. Partridge has a splendidly absurd sequence here, which I hope I may be allowed to follow, though it makes a slight digression. As Volpone is expecting to enjoy Celia soon after his chat with Mosca, another danger from the visit of Lady Would-be occurs to him:

> I fear
> Another hell too, that my loathing this
> Will quite expel my appetite to the other.

Mr. Partridge finds here a striking piece of symbolism: "Hell, to this animal, means a loss of appetite; heaven, a gratifying of it." A more refined type of man, I readily agree with my brother critic, would have found his heaven in hearing from Lady Would-be the type of lecture that we both give. But shortly afterwards Mr. Partridge has an opposite complaint against Volpone, who remarks to Mosca, in a moment of triumph after cheating an old miser, that "the pleasure of all womankind's not in it":

> Here is the perfect perversion of the sexual instinct. Greed and
> vanity and a debased intelligence have so far debased his normal
> instincts that the joy of life comes not from giving joy to others
> but from giving pain.

At least, then, the animal is no longer blamed for being sunk in his instincts, and incapable of the pleasures of the human mind. But also, Volpone intends a hyperbole; he thinks well of the pleasure to be gained from womankind, and uses this to say that the moral pleasure to be gained from penalising a corrupt grandee is especially great. Compassionate Mr. Partridge himself, and moral Ben Jonson too, and the whole audience so far as they can be won over, are all committed to this same line of interest, even if it is true that they had better have stayed in bed with their wives. The denunciation is thus particularly absurd here, but also it distracts attention from the main point, that Volpone is designed to work as a contact-man, sufficiently at home with the London audience to show them Venice.

Naturally, for this purpose he must also be at home in Venice, and there need to be moments when he behaves with a convincing amount of native wickedness. To make him absurd is then the only way to save his popularity, and this is unflinchingly done. The main case is the attempted rape of Celia; traditionally he has been found absurd enough there not to revolt a predominantly male audience, though I have never found it possible to alter the mind of a female student who already considered him a monster. Rape is even more unpopular in the theatre than elsewhere, and the incident is a direct cause of the downfall of Volpone; delicate handling is required. Volpone first loves Celia on hearsay only; her beauty is reported by Mosca, in a handsome speech—he must have been told to scout round; it is part of the vanity of Volpone to enjoy the greatest beauties. But also to win their hearts; it does not occur to him that she might *want* to refuse him— to that extent, the attempted rape is merely a technical one. To find the rich old husband willing to sell her, instead of having to be cheated, was a great extra pleasure for Volpone; it showed he deserved to be cheated even more than Volpone had supposed. The lady herself, he still assumed, he could woo with his real charms, chief among them his poetic imagination. I am not sure what Jonson felt about this, or meant the audience to feel, but I expect he considered the behaviour of Volpone straightforward. He offers Celia classical charades in expensive fancy dress, and a modern reader is not surprised when she treats his speeches as merely gabble adding to her torment. But Jonson himself had just discovered that he could handle the Court by this method, and win a comfortable life by it for a long while. I expect he could hardly imagine wooing a lady in any other way. And then again, there is a rather puzzling wholeheartedness in the lyrical effect when Volpone offers Celia

> A diamond, would have bought Lollia Paulina
> When she came in like starlight, hid with jewels.

Puzzling, I mean, if you assume that Jonson despised his characters for feeling this kind of enthusiasm. I think he felt it himself very readily. The phrase here is easily turned into contempt, because only a very ugly woman could need to be totally hidden behind her jewellery; but the poet writes with the genuine bated breath of the crowd standing outside to watch the great ladies make their entries. Lollia achieved mention for her splendour during the days of Augustus; and Jonson, it seems to me, like a number of earlier Renaissance scholars, admired Imperial Rome in a way which we now find remote. He thought that modern science was just beginning to get us back to that paradise, that magnificent technology which had somehow got lost in the Dark Ages; he is helping to recover our birthright when he imagines unheard of luxuries. (This assumption that he too was complaining against science for being irreligious is therefore peculiarly absurd.) Indeed, the whole story of Volpone is in a way a compliment to seventeenth-century Venice, because it was recognisably borrowed from Imperial Rome.

Whether attractive or not, the wooing fails because of the simple piety of the girl, who had already accepted misery when her father sold her to a rich cripple. With needling pathos, Celia makes any offer she can think of to Volpone if only he will spare her virtue, and of course she will then also "report him virtuous." This has an electric effect, because, as the audience is expected to realise, he has been operating all along from a peculiar code of honour:

> VOLPONE: Think me cold
> Frozen, and impotent, and so report me?

Such is the threat which forces him to lay hands upon her, and the virtuous young man at once bounds out of hiding to interrupt him. Since this young man has also learned a more important secret, that Volpone is not dying and only pretends it to win legacies, Volpone is next found bemoaning to Mosca the prospect of "beggary and infamy." But surely it was not a reputation for sexual potency which he has been building up for the last three years by pretending to be at death's door? The audience liked hearing about absurd points of honour, and here they are given a specially absurd one; then Volpone and Mosca go into a childish huddle for comfort, confessing and making excuses to one another. It amounts to a fairly elaborate protection for Volpone, to prevent the audience from swinging against him.

Mosca seems an undeveloped character, but this is not a fault of the author, nor yet an illustration of a profound theory that all characters ought to be undeveloped. One might indeed complain that one or two of Mosca's comments are too magnificent to belong to him:

> Bountiful bones! What horrid strange offence
> Did he commit 'gainst nature, in his youth,
> Worthy this age?

(that is, making him deserve to become this horrible old man); but such rhetoric can be viewed as simply imitated from his master, for whose feelings he has a real sympathy; also, it helps to keep up a uniformity of tone. Apart from that, the plot requires Mosca to be a conventional-minded parasite, actually *trying* to be a "typical" one, because this is what causes his downfall. At the start of act 3, the correct point for the "crisis" of the design, he tells us what a clever parasite he is, and we find at once that he has overplayed his hand. He planted the good young man as a witness to something else, but events move too fast, and now the witness knows that Volpone is not dying. Disaster is only averted by the splendid impudence of Mosca at the trial, aided by the contemptible behaviour of the misers; but the nerve of Volpone is shaken by having to appear in court, and this causes his fatal error, which begins act 5. After being carried home, he looks round for a yet more reckless action, to recover his nerve:

> 'Fore God, my left leg 'gan to have the cramp,
> And I apprehended straight some power had struck me
> With a dead palsy. Well, I must be merry

—or fear will give him a disease; so he drinks, and as usual on the stage the effect is immediate:

> Tis almost gone, already; I shall conquer.
> Any device now, of a rare ingenious knavery
> That would possess me with a violent laughter
> Would make me up again.

That is, not only his chief pleasure, but his basic confidence, his assurance that his view of the scene around him is correct, comes from being able to fool in a spectacular manner these great world bankers, so as to prove that he completely understands their folly. It is plain here that Jonson was not still operating on the crude theory about "humours" which he had used earlier while struggling and frustrated. Unless you accept Volpone as an unusual character, almost as complicated as those of Shakespeare which the same audience enjoyed, the story if merely incredible. Be this as it may, after Volpone and Mosca have boasted together a little, tenderly though Mosca rallies him a bit to calm his fears, he signs a will leaving Mosca his entire fortune and tells Mosca to announce that he is dead. It is done with no expectation of further gain, merely to torment the expectant misers and induce them to act still more absurdly. Mosca comes to feel uneasy about this, after dismissing three misers with insults one after another, while he works away at his accounts and Volpone (like the author as usual) peers delightedly from the wings; Mosca suspects that they may feel too insulted to continue the arrangement after the truth becomes known; but Volpone feels certain that they will swallow any insult to get his fortune.

As it happens, then, what destroys Volpone is a superstitious fear, while on trial in court, that he has been genuinely made a cripple by "some power," the guardian angel of the state of Venice presumably. This would recall to early audiences the corresponding movement in the mind of Macbeth, whose throat had become so dry while murdering Duncan that he found he could not say "Amen" when the guard said "God bless us." But why couldn't he? he asks his wife with his unnerving self-pity, while it is obvious that he was lucky to be unable to betray his presence. I think that Johson copied this detail from Shakespeare's play, which had only just been brought out, merely because he considered it true to life—another bit of evidence that *Macbeth* was written before *King Lear*. But the dating does no affect the present argument; I only say that, as the mind of Volpone was so close to the mind of Macbeth, at a crucial point which would be recognised by the Globe audiences, they cannot have regarded him simply as a Humour.

After the third miser has been sent away with a flea in his ear, Volpone bounds out of hiding and takes the final step which ensures disaster:

> VOLPONE: Bid him eat lettuce well. My witty mischief,
> Let me embrace thee. O that I could now
> Transform thee to a Venus!—Mosca, go
> Straight take my habit of clarissimo
> And walk the streets; be seen, torment them more;
> We must pursue, as well as plot. Who would
> Have lost this feast?

The difficult rhythm of the last sentence, addressed directly to the audience, is best treated as a vast sigh of content.

> VOLPONE: That I could but now think of some disguise
> To meet 'em in, and ask 'em questions;
> How I would vex 'em still at every turn!
> MOSCA: Sir, I can fit you.
> VOLPONE: Canst thou?
> MOSCA: Yes. I know
> One of the commandatori, sir, so like you.
> Him will I straight make drunk, and bring you his habit.

Thus Volpone will be outside, disguised as a humble policeman, with his servants assured that he is dead and taking orders from his accredited heir. He might induce them to recognise him, but this would be at the cost of admitting that he was not at the point of death, which would lose him the three legacies. He is handing Mosca the ideal situation to betray him (exposing a servant to temptation, as my mother used to say). Indeed, Mosca might claim later to have only protected Volpone's interests by refusing to recognise him. But Mosca seems to look at him as a chess player might do at an opponent who is sacrificing his queen: "Did you really mean to do that? Well, I must take the obvious advantage, whatever you have in mind"; so he captures the queen. At first he only demands half, but when Volpone rejects this with indignation he becomes absorbed in the fun of trickery and conflict—he has no idea that he is breaking Volpone's heart, or at least exasperating the pride which in a Venetian grandee is even more dangerous. In the final trial, he orders Volpone the supposed policeman to be whipped for insolence to himself, now in Volpone's place; perhaps he feels that the extravagance of the presumption makes him safe, because no one could suspect he is doing it. Jonson is careful not to let the farce become weepy at the climax, and Volpone merely asks the audience to agree with him that "if I confess, it cannot be much worse"; but it is, and the real reason why he chooses to confess is that he has nothing left to live for, and would prefer to be wronged under his own high name. As he abandons his disguise Mosca gives a last whimpering cry of "Why, patron!"; he had not believed that anything could make the father-figure turn against him. The court of Venice is shown as grossly venal, and naturally outraged by flippancy about wills; it orders Volpone to be crippled by irons till he is as decrepit as he has pretended to be. He is led out with the grim stoical last line, faintly reminiscent of Iago, "This is called mortifying of a fox." It sounds as if some practical operation was called that, but I do not know what.

It has been argued that the play is the Tragedy of Volpone, and this question largely turns on whether you decide that Mosca has broken his heart. A lady student pointed out to me that Mosca, when Volpone tells him to invent an excuse for not showing his supposed corpse, answers stoutly: "I'll say it stunk, sir." Considering what the pretence has been, this is the correct excuse, and Mosca evidently enjoys his work on the whole; but an actor could fairly present him as getting tired of being hugged and kissed all the time. Jonson himself might tell the actor to do it, since his feelings on the subject were mixed. As one often finds with manly men, who need pleasure with coarse vigorous women (and resent the pretentions of ladies), he was very susceptible to elegant courageous lads, and inclined to denounce sodomy in other people so as to cover this up. But the English audience expected sodomy in raffish Italians, and Jonson does not treat the matter as at all crucial. Another conviction of the first audience would be more decisive for the motivation: that the rulers of Venice are immensely proud aristocrats, though of course all "in trade." Jonson was no good at presenting aristocratic dignity, any more than romantic love, and preferred to take the mickey out of them, but he could rely on his audience to presume that Volpone, though a rebel, kept his class pride; and as this supplies his motive a modern producer should put it back. Telling the audience that Mosca is no use for pleasure ("O that I could") cannot be intended to forestall scandal because it is delayed till the last act—it comes just before their feelings for one another become decisive. I think its function is to make clear that this love is of a comparatively dignified kind, the love of a criminal for his accomplice to whom he boasts, nobly undemanding in any other way; but it is still doomed, especially in a man with a code of pride.

You may have noticed that my last paragraph set out to shoo away the feeling of tragedy but ended by yielding to it. I have next to recall the real end of the play. Some of my readers can perhaps remember (long, long ago) seeing *Peter Pan*, in which Tinker Bell, though dying of poison, will recover if the audience believes in fairies—"clap if you do." Tired of sitting still, the children save the life of Tinker Bell every time. This device had presumably been learned from the end of the *Beggar's Opera*, which also allows the audience to give a reprieve. In *Peter Pan* they are only asked to confess a habit of daydreaming, I think; but in the *Beggar's Opera* the first audiences were asked to confess that they were half on the side of the rebels, they half agreed that they ought to overthrow the Government of Walpole. It was a display of careless ease, but the call for applause was bound to have a certain fighting political point. This in turn had been taken from *Volpone*, one of the few Jacobean plays which were still revived; and there, I think, in its rough prejudiced way, the device amounted to a vote for English law against Continental law. The English had long been proud that their legal procedure did not admit torture (Shakespeare uses the belief, with the vagueness that was needed, at *2 Henry VI*, 3.1.120); and indeed Volpone could hardly even be detained under English law, except for masquerading as a policeman. You are not asked to believe that Volpone is a good character, but that the wicked laws of Venice inherently produce characters like him—and like Shylock, for that matter. No English audience would want to cripple Volpone, as the Venetian bench did, for making Venice ridiculous; they can be trusted to let him off, thus dispelling the clouds of tragedy which have gathered over the last act, from the intensity of the reactions of these odd characters. Jonson invented the device, likely enough, just to preserve decorum; to make the farce end like a farce though it had become so gripping. All the same, the pardon of Volpone is given the dignity of political language, and some members of the first audience would be likely to take it seriously. Our moralizing school, on the other hand, cannot face the actual end of the play; such critics hardly ever admit its existence:

> though the Fox be punished by the laws,
> He yet doth hope, there is no suffering due
> For any fault which he hath done 'gainst you.
> If there be, censure him; here he doubtful stands.
> If not, fare jovially, and clap your hands.

Better results really might be expected, morally as well as aesthetically, if they would fare more jovially.

The False Ending in *Volpone*

Stephen Greenblatt

This essay aims at exploring Jonson's use in *Volpone* of a characteristic formal device of Elizabethan and Jacobean drama, and of his own plays in particular, the false ending. At the close of act 4, Volpone has completely triumphed: Celia and Bonario have been led off to await sentencing as adulterers and slanderers; the gulls believe more than ever that Volpone is dying; even the law court—sole seat of authority and justice within the world of the play—has been duped. If we yet feel that the innocent cannot be left to suffer, it is in this play only a vague and conventional sentiment.

The force of this "ending" should not be underestimated in reading the drama, as indeed it cannot be in performance. For *Volpone* up to this point has been an enormously *busy* play. The stage has been filled with frenetic activity: endless plotting, self-transformations, narrow escapes, hucksterism, sadistic jokes, attempted rape. Like the mountebank's patter, there have been almost no pauses: one monstrous manifestation of greed and low cunning is no sooner out the door than another pushes in to Volpone's chamber. And the language of the play fully reinforces this busyness and profusion. In keeping with the characters' obsession with wealth, there is an extraordinarily detailed "thingness" in their speech: pills of butter, Romagnia and rich Candian wines. Lombard's vinegar, nativity pie, furs and footcloths, bright chequins, plate, pearls, musk-melons, pome-citrons, Colchester oysters, Selsey cockles, sheep's gall, roasted bitch's marrow, sod earwigs, pounded caterpillars, capon's grease, fasting spittle,

From the *Journal of English and Germanic Philology* 75, nos. 1 & 2 (January–April 1976). © 1976 by the Board of Trustees of the University of Illinois.

flayed apes, brains of peacocks, and so on, and so on. This is a play of lists, recipes, and catalogues; even Volpone's attempted seduction of Celia has the ring of an exotic inventory:

> Thy bathes shall be in the iuyce of iuly-flowres,
> Spirit of roses, and of violets,
> The milke of vnicornes, and panthers breath
> Gather'd in bagges, and mixt with *cretran* wines.
> Our drinke shall be prepared gold, and amber;
> Which we will take, vntill my roofe whirle round
> With the *vertigo:* and my dwarfe shall dance,
> My eunuch sing, my foole make vp the antique.
> Whil'st, we, in changed shapes, act OVIDS tales,
> Thou, like EVROPA now, and I like IOVE,
> Then I like MARS, and thou like ERYCINE,
> So, of the rest, till we haue quite run through
> And weary'd all the fables of the gods.
>
> (3.7.213–25)

Profusion in Shakespeare creates, in Yeats's expressive phrase, "the emotion of multitude," the sense that the whole cosmos is involved in the action of the play. In *Volpone,* instead of the emotion of multitude we have precisely the avoidance of depth in a vertiginous swirl of words. Volpone's speech, like the actions he generates, must flow on without pause, for in silence lurks the hidden meaning of his words, the anxiety of "run through" and "weary'd." And we, in the audience, participate in this flow, for we do not want Volpone to stop, any more than the crowd at a circus wants the tightrope walker to fall, though its enjoyment is predicated on that possibility.

Volpone's act culminates in the first trial scene. The latter half of act 4 has the feeling of a finale: up to now, great care has been taken to keep the gulls apart; at last they have all gathered together in the courtroom. We are reminded of the close of *Every Man in His Humour:* the isolated monads, locked in their own egotism and scheming, are brought together before the seat of judgment. This sense of an ending is compounded by the movement from darkness to light; Volpone is forced to perform the part of an invalid not in the convenient obscurity of his bedroom but in the glare of the Scrutineo. Jonson himself in the *Discoveries* provides the perfect description of the situation: *"Truth* and *Goodnesse* are plaine and open: but, *Imposture* is ever asham'd of the light. A Puppet-play must be shadow'd, and seene in the darke; for draw the Curtaine, *Et sordet gesticulatio."* The play metaphor here serves to remind us that what is at stake in the trial scene is not simply Volpone's con-game but the principle of theatrical illusion on which it is based. As all of our enjoyment has been derived from that illusion, we may dread its exposure before the judges, but we deem that exposure an inflexible rule of the moral universe: *"Imposture is ever asham'd of the light."* But in act 4 of *Volpone,* imposture unexpectedly triumphs: judgment fails, the innocent are condemned, and the fox is set free.

What is the effect on this "finale"? For a moment, Jonson offers the audience a resolution precisely the reverse of the one he will finally provide. It is as if he were testing the spectators, forcing them to reexamine their own sympathies: "You have identified with Volpone, enjoyed his machinations, taken his part against his victims, even the virtuous but vapid Celia and Bonario. All right, I give you Volpone's triumph." The audience must ask itself, "What would a world be like in which Volpone has triumphed?" In reply, it wills Volpone's ultimate downfall. The spectators do not know exactly why they insist that the play continue—they scarcely have time to analyze their responses—but they do not applaud and they do not move for the exits. The victory they longed for has the taste of ashes.

Jonson's source for this brilliant device is probably Marlowe's *Jew of Malta,* in which we find a similar, if cruder, situation. Thrown over the walls "To be a prey for vultures and wild beasts" (5.1.59), Barabas lies for a moment as if dead and then pops up like a toy that rights itself no matter how often it is floored. With the aid of the Turks who conveniently arrive at that precise moment, the Jew unexpectedly triumphs over his enemies. As the Christians are led away in chains, the audience is given a momentary vision of an ending diametrically opposed to the one they finally see: Barabas's "I now am Governor of Malta."

In both Marlowe's play and Jonson's, then, there is the same structural pattern: a near defeat (anticipating the true finale) and a false triumph. But there is an important difference. In *Volpone,* as we shall see, there is a highly significant pause before the plot resumes; Marlowe's hero scarcely pauses for breath. Barabas's declaration of triumph does not even fill out the line. The last syllable—"true"—marks the decisive turn toward those events that will finally destroy him:

> I now am Governor of Malta; true,
> But Malta hates me, and in hating me
> My life's in danger, and what boots it thee
> Poor Barabas, to be the Governor,

> When as thy life shall be at their command?
> No, Barabas, this must be looked into;
> And since by wrong thou got'st authority,
> Maintain it bravely by firm policy,
> At least unprofitably lose it not.
>
> (5.2.30–38)

Whatever reasons Barabas may offer here for doing so, the audience *expects* him immediately to divest himself of the governorship; the space that he has carved out for himself to bustle in is defined precisely by his isolation. Thus when he rises from the dead, his first words reveal the essential condition of his existence: "What, all alone? " (5.1.61). Significantly, it is in the moments just prior to this resurrection, rather than in the moments following his victory, that the audience is given time to ask itself questions: not, "what would a world be like in which Barabas has triumphed?" but "what would a world be like without Barabas?" In *The Jew of Malta,* the audience wills not the hero's downfall, but his return to life.

In Jonson's play, the crucial pause occurs *after* Volpone's triumph. As Dryden noted, "there appear two actions in the play; the first naturally ending with the fourth act; the second forced from it in the fifth." At the close of act 4, the stage clears and must for a moment at least be completely bare, until Volpone enters, now safely back in his house. Where Barabas's speech after his triumph had slurred over the similar structural break, Volpone's calls attention to it: "Well, I am here; and all this brunt is past" (5.1.1). What is striking about this monosyllabic line—and about the entire opening of act 5—is its *deadness.* Volpone throughout has been a master of the alchemy of language, transforming vulgar wealth into precious wonders, but suddenly his powers fail him. This must be one of the rare instances in the history of the drama in which the author's genius is manifested in the collapse of his verse. The deadness has all along been lurking just beneath the glittering surface of Volpone's existence, and now in the pause after the Fox's triumph, it is revealed. We suddenly glimpse that dark thing which lay hidden behind all of the frenetic activity—not criminality or satanic evil but something subtler and more insidious: emptiness, boredom, the void.

In the flatness of these scenes—the flatness which prompts Mosca's superficially solicitous but deeply ironic "You are not taken with it, enough, me thinks?"—we fully understand for the first time the meaning of Volpone's extraordinary energy, as we glimpse the void which that energy has been struggling to fill. What we perceive, I suggest, are those vast spaces that opened up on both a physical and psychological plane in the Renaissance. Heirs of nineteenth-century liberalism, we think of this expansion as a triumph of the human spirit, a breakthrough into the light, an awakening:

> Man [in the Middle Ages] was conscious of himself only as member of a race, people, party, family, or corporation—only through some general category. In Italy this veil first melted into air; an *objective* treatment and consideration of the State and of all the things of this world became possible. The *subjective* side at the same time asserted itself with corresponding emphasis; man became a spiritual *individual,* and recognized himself as such.

"This veil first melted into air"—how optimistic Burckhardt sounds! And indeed Volpone seems to strive heroically to bear out this optimism. He is preeminently a man no longer "conscious of himself only as member of a race, people, party, family, or corporation":

> What should I doe,
> But cocker vp my *genius,* and liue free
> To all delights, my fortune calls me to?
> I haue no wife, no parent, child, allie,
> To giue my substance to; but whom I make,
> Must be my heire: and this makes men obserue me.
>   (1.1.70–75)

Volpone speaks about himself and to himself here with that odd combination of engagement and detachment that characterizes most Western self-consciousness from precisely this period to the present time. He achieves the jaunty self-regard exuded by that virtual slogan of Renaissance confidence, "cocker vp my *genius,* and liue free," by regarding himself from the outside, by looking through the eyes of those who observe him. Because we ourselves live in just this way, because we are, ironically enough, Volpone's heirs, we are not fully conscious of the remarkable process occurring in these lines, though it determines the shape and meaning of the whole play: Volpone transforms himself into a theater in which he is both actor and audience. Of course, he plays for others as well, for the whole flock of gulls, but he would not be able to function at all had he not first performed the act of theatrical self-consciousness manifested here. He hears what he sounds like, sees what he looks like to others; and he can do so only because he has taken the others into himself. Moreover, he has separated himself off from himself, so that he can perform operations upon his own being.

"Our bodies are our gardens, to the which our wills are gardeners": the speaker is Iago, but the principle is Volpone's as well.

For ourselves, as I have suggested, this kind of self-consciousness is all but automatic, so much so that we are lured into a belief that its development is "natural," that we inevitably grow into our peculiar way of regarding and manipulating our identities. Indeed, an influential modern social psychologist like George Herbert Mead assures us that only by forming within ourselves a "generalized other"—a kind of permanent, nonpaying theater audience that judges all our thoughts and actions—do we develop a "complete self." But in *Volpone,* the fashioning of this theatrical self, at once detached and committed, has the air of something original and willed, just as Volpone seems deliberately to will that adoration of gold which comes "naturally" to most men. Part of the contemporary fascination of Jonson's play is precisely that we feel ourselves present at the very fountainhead of modern consciousness, present just as the decisive, formative steps in the direction of our own minds are being taken. And we see that these steps are not natural or inevitable; we are invited rather to view them with mingled attraction and repulsion.

Volpone is consummately a man who has created his own identity, fashioned parts for himself which he proceeds to play with all the technical skills of a fine actor. Liberated from any hierarchy in the universe which would impose limits on his being, dependent only upon his own powerful imagination, he seems freer than anyone in his world. Indeed, with his ready disguises, he is liberated even from himself, uncommitted to a single, fixed role. He has the energy of Proteus. Yet in the lull following the false ending, we perceive the converse, as it were, of this spendid energy, a yawning emptiness which at once permits its flowering and swallows it up. "We are all hollow and empty," wrote Montaigne (in "Of Glory"): "It is not with wind and sound that we have to fill ourselves; we need more solid substance to repair us."

The essential action of *Volpone*—thrown into relief by its momentary collapse at the start of act 5—is the hero's attempt to "fill himself." It is thus that he embarks on his endless accumulations of things, the items inventoried in such loving detail by Mosca as the gulls frantically question him about his master's will: Turkey carpets, nine; two suits of bedding, tissue; of cloth of gold, two more; of several vellets, eight; eight chests of linen; six chests of diaper, four of damask; down-beds, and bolsters; ten suits of hangings; two cabinets, one of ebony, the other, mother of pearl; one salt of agate, a perfumed box made of onyx, and so forth. There is something heroic about this relentless acquisitiveness. But no matter how many things he may amass, the space is never filled; its outer boundaries keep receding into the darkness.

If Volpone has no limiting relationships, by the same token he has no authentic relationships. He is alone. His condition epitomizes that isolation which obsesses the great seventeenth-century writers, the sense that man has lost any immediate relationship to the order of the world, the feeling that he is no longer enclosed in a web of sympathetic intercommunication linking all created things. "I haue no wife, no parent, child, allie, / To giue my substance to"—he is cut off from the past (parent), the present (wife), the future (child), and the society of men. And what of his "substance"? The succeeding lines make clear that Volpone intends by this word his wealth, all of the gold and jewels he has been amassing. But "substance" has an odd animation, an effect like that we find so often in Dickens: Volpone's wealth is intermingled with his name, his identity, that whole complex being one would share with others. Volpone's substance is his alone; this is the very condition and principle of his freedom. And if this autonomy transforms time into a theater in which he can act, it also means that for Volpone time does not offer the assurance of continuity. He is vouchsafed only a vision of a temporal void still more vast than the spatial:

> Sunnes, that set, may rise againe:
> But if, once, we lose this light,
> 'Tis with vs perpetuall night.
> (3.7.171–73)

Catallus to the contrary, sexual pleasure does not relieve Volpone's solitude; indeed there is a distinctly hollow note in his professions of desire, marked by his lapse into literary parody:

> But angry CVPID, bolting from her eyes,
> Hath shot himselfe into me, like a flame;
> Where, now, he flings about his burning heat,
> As in a fornace, an ambitious fire,
> Whose vent is stopt.
> (2.4.3–7)

The deliberate grossness of the final words mocks the poetic convention, but expresses no more genuine passion than "My liuer melts" a few lines further on. It is not simply in order to deceive the judges that Volpone is brought into court "as impotent"; this has been a buried suggestion throughout the play. When Lady Would-be appears instead of Celia, Volpone fears "that my loathing this / Will quite expell my appetite to the other"

(3.3.28–29). And even his great seduction speech, with its vision of endless self-metamorphoses in the service of erotic excitement, suggests sexual anxiety, the fear already noted in those disturbing words "run through" and "weary'd."

The succession of masks Volpone offers Celia are an attempt to stave off the boredom that follows hard on a voluptuary's pleasure. They aim at a continual arousal, so as to prevent any dull pause between moments of satiety. In other words, like the plate, jewels, and bright chequins, they are an attempt to fill a void, here not a physical space but the dark gap between discontinuous experiences. The "changed shapes" Volpone lovingly describes—

> some sprightly dame of *France*,
> Braue *Tuscan* lady, or proud *Spanish* beauty;
> Sometimes vnto the *Persian Sophies* wife;
> Or the grand-*Signiors* mistresse; and, for change,
> To one of our most art-full courtizans,
> Or some quick *Negro*, or cold *Russian*
> (3.7.227–32)

—are, in a sense, more important than sexual gratification itself, since that gratification is always succeeded by a pause. It is as if Volpone has displaced his sexual energy from its usual instinctual object onto masquerading. Indeed in the lull after the courtroom triumph, he openly acknowledges his preference:

> MOSCA: You are not taken with it, enough, me thinks?
> VOLPONE: O, more, then if I had enjoy'd the wench:
> The pleasure of all woman-kind's not like it.
> (5.2.9–11)

But if, as I have suggested, the erotic masks are calculated to fill the gaps between points of time and thus to achieve a kind of timelessness, they are doomed to failure. For beneath the masquerade, time is secretly at work, bearing men toward old age and oblivion. The destructive effects of time are vividly manifested in the horrible old miser, Corbaccio, on whom Volpone muses:

> So many cares, so many maladies,
> So many feares attending on old age,
> Yea, death so often call'd on, as no wish
> Can be more frequent with 'hem, their limbs faint,

> Their senses dull, their seeing, hearing, going,
> All dead before them; yea, their very teeth,
> Their instruments of eating, fayling them:
> Yet this is reckon'd life! Nay, here was one,
> Is now gone home, that wishes to liue longer!
> Feeles not his gout, nor palsie, faines himselfe
> Yonger, by scores of yeeres, flatters his age,
> With confident belying it, hopes he may
> With charmes, like AESON, haue his youth restor'd:
> And with these thoughts so battens, as if fate
> Would be as easily cheated on, as he,   *Another knocks.*
> And all turnes aire!
>
> (1.4.144–59)

This is a strange and revealing moment: we expect derision, but the tone of the speech is more complex, mingling scorn, wonder, and a deep fear. The knock on the door—merely another gull presenting himself—has an eerie effect, like the sound of a string snapping, slowly and sadly dying away, in *The Cherry Orchard. All turnes air!*—for a brief moment we glimpse that void which is perceived again more powerfully at the false ending, that sense of emptiness against which Volpone struggles. Once again, he attempts to cheat or at least to mock this vision through disguise, the disguise which enacts every one of the horrors of age on which he had brooded. "An old, decrepit wretch," Corvino describes Volpone, as Volpone had described Corbaccio,

> That ha's no sense, no sinew; takes his meate
> With others fingers; onely knowes to gape,
> When you doe scald his gummes; a voice; a shadow.
>
> (3.7.42–45)

By pretending to be old, sick, and dying, Volpone transforms time into a mere fiction of time. But to the extent to which he succeeds, he commits himself to living in a fiction, a "waking dreame"(1.1.18).

Volpone's relationships with the other characters are tinged with the same unreality. To be sure, he appears unmasked with Mosca and indeed speaks with an affection that borders on love: "My beloued MOSCA"; "Excellent MOSCA! / Come hither, let me kisse thee"; "I cannot hold; good rascall, let me kisse thee"; "Let me embrace thee. O, that I could now / Transforme thee to a VENVS." But in their dialogues Jonson brilliantly suggests Volpone's fundamental incomprehension of the existence of a consciousness other than his own:

> VOLPONE: Dispatch, dispatch: I long to haue possession
>   Of my new present.
> MOSCA: That, and thousands more,
>   I hope, to see you lord of.
> VOLPONE: Thankes, kind MOSCA.
> MOSCA: And that, when I am lost in blended dust,
>   And hundred such, as I am, in succession—
> VOLPONE: Nay, that were too much, MOSCA.
> MOSCA: You shall liue,
>   Still, to delude these *harpyies*.
> VOLPONE: Louing MOSCA.
>   (1.2.116–22)

Mosca's bitter self-consciousness is more than matched by Volpone's anaesthetized egotism.

If Volpone, in his theatrical self-consciousness, has absorbed the other characters into himself, he has, through that very process, "unrealized" them and created them anew, as a playwright creates his characters. There is something at once spurious and pathetic in Volpone's observation of his victims' reaction to his "death":

> Now, they begin to flutter:
> They neuer thinke of me. Looke, see, see, see!
>   (5.3.16–17)

He has after all fashioned all of the conditions of their response. Of course we delight in the cheating of the scavengers who hover about what they think is a dying man; we share in the sadistic pleasure Volpone so frankly offers:

> Letting the cherry knock against their lips,
> And, draw it, by their mouths, and back againe.
>   (1.1.89–90)

But here again the false ending serves to focus our latent perception of the limitations of such pleasure. Volpone's sadism has no power to sustain itself, to build anything lasting; the moment the gulling ceases, the pleasure utterly vanishes.

In committing himself to a fictive existence, a life of masks and pseudo-relationships, Volpone cuts himself off from the experience of duration. He must renew himself each moment—as Mosca renews his patron's makeup—lest the whole performance simply cease and vanish. Saint Augustine had written, in a phrase on which Renaissance thinkers meditated, that if God "were to withdraw what we may call his 'constructive power' from existing things, they would cease to exist, just as they did not exist before they were made." Jonson's play is, as it were, a demonic imitation of such a universe, with Volpone replacing God as the agent of continual creation. Should his energy lapse for an instant, his world would collapse and he would fall into nothingness. Such a collapse is precisely what is threatened— in theatrical rather than philosophical terms—in the aftermath of the court-room triumph. For a moment, we are allowed to feel, within the play itself, the emptiness of the stage after the performance is over. And even when the stage is reanimated by the presence of Mosca and Volpone, their dialogue is the backstage chatter of actors after the play is done:

> MOSCA: 'T seem'd to mee, you sweat, sir.
> VOLPONE: In troth, I did a little.
>
> (5.2.37–38)

At the start of act 5, then, Volpone is in the surrealistic situation of a character who has somehow survived his play. He has no plot to sustain him, no external guarantees of duration. For an instant during the trial, he recalls nervously, he thought he had lost the very essence of his theatrical existence—his mimetic power:

> 'Fore god, my left legge 'gan to haue the crampe;
> And I apprehended, straight, some power had strooke me
> With a dead palsey.
>
> (5.1.5–7)

There is nothing in the play to make us believe that the "power" Volpone suddenly fears is anything but an illusion, a superstitious projection. The threat here is not the supernatural but the physical: the fear of real paralysis in place of feigned. The "dead palsey" is the radical antithesis of that transcendence of the body which an exultant Mosca celebrates as the highest achievement of a successful parasite like himself:

> But your fine, elegant rascall, that can rise,
> And stoope (almost together) like an arrow;
> Shoot through the aire, as nimbly as a starre;
> Turne short, as cloth a swallow; and be here,
> And there, and here, and yonder, all at once;
> Present to any humour, all occasion;
> And change a visor, swifter, then a thought!
> This is the creature, had the art borne with him.
>
> (3.1.23–30)

The creature who can perform these feats has literally to be nothing, a bodiless fiction. Hence the terror lurking in a mere cramp: a sign that the body resists the will and thus that the fiction is collapsing. For Volpone, to sense the body's resistance is to sense death.

On regaining his lair at the start of act 5, Volpone's first response is to call for "a boule of lustie wine" to chase away the cold deadness at his center: "This heate is life," he declares after drinking. But wine is obviously not enough. As he himself suggest, he will continue to exist only if he can somehow regenerate the plot:

> Any deuice, now, of rare, ingenious knauery,
> That would possesse me with a violent laughter,
> Would make me vp, againe!
>
> (5.1.14–16)

In Volpone's world—the world of continual creation—to stand still is to vanish. It is thus that Mosca, employing the simplest negative psychology, pushes his patron towards his fatal misstep:

> We must, here, be fixt;
> Here, we must rest; this is our master-peece:
> We cannot thinke, to goe beyond this.
>
> (5.2.12–14)

Of course, Volpone's great fear is to be fixed, to be struck, as it were, with a dead palsey. He must think "to goe beyond this"; otherwise he and the play simply end.

The device he chooses to make himself up again is to give out that he is dead. This is, in a sense, the supreme triumph of Volpone's art, for his strategy is to turn what he fears into fiction, and what he fears most of all is death. But at this point, Mosca intervenes, in an attempt to trap Volpone in this ultimate masquerade and establish himself permanently in his own new part, that of Volpone's heir. And with this attempt to freeze the roles, the whole elaborate charade collapses.

Significantly, at the true end of the play, Mosca and Volpone are both condemned to be "fixed," the former as a perpetual prisoner in the galleys and the latter still more tightly:

> since the most was gotten by imposture,
> By faining lame, gout, palsey, and such diseases,
> Thou art to lie in prison, crampt with irons,
> Till thou bee'st sicke, and lame indeed.
>
> (5.12.121–24)

"Crampt with irons"— like Proteus, Volpone will be held fast until all metamorphoses cease. Or rather he will be permitted one last, bitter metamorphosis, until his being finally and irrevocably assumes the shape of his mask.

The assault on metamorphosis strikes not only at Volpone as a character but at the whole world which he has brought into being in the opening moments of the play. As one may say that Lear symbolically kills Cordelia in the first scene and spends the rest of the play enduring the consequences of his action, so as the curtain rises Volpone performs the determining action of the play: he ritually displaces God from the center of the universe. From this primal displacement flow all of the subsequent transformations; from it too derive those vast spaces, in both the world and the self, which the transformations strive vainly to fill.

Perhaps this has too orthodox a ring. There is at least a suggestion, I believe, that the seeds of Volpone's downfall lie not in his displacement of God but in the play-world itself, in a universe with no guarantees of continuity. From this perspective, it does not matter whether the agent of creation is God, or gold, or the artist; the scheme of things itself is wrong. After all, the finale of Volpone does not attempt to replace God in the central position; indeed the corruption of the judges undermines even the more modest conclusion that Justice has triumphed. What the fettering of Volpone and Mosca does accomplish is to end the play, to destroy that principle whereby not only these characters but any dramatic characters exist. If at the false ending Jonson keeps the audience in their seats and thus proves that Volpone's triumph is empty, so at the true ending, he makes part of the meaning of the work the audience's exit from the playhouse. He directs the audience, as it were, to reject the theatrical principles of displacement, mask, and metamorphosis.

That this rejection cut very deep for Jonson himself is suggested, above all, in the scene in which Volpone masquerades as Scoto of Mantua. The real Scoto was a professional actor, leader of a company licensed by the Duke of Mantua, and Volpone's Scoto is also a kind of playwright-actor, mounting his bank to perform for the rabble. In his astonishing verbal facility, his bombastic defensiveness, his proud boast that he has "past the craggie pathes of studie, and come to the flowrie plaines of honour, and reputation" (2.2.169–70), and even in the incidental details of his career, Volpone's Scoto seems to be a striking parody of Jonson himself. Alvin Kernan, who has noted the many parallels, suggests (in his edition on *Volpone*) that Jonson is working to distinguish false art from true: "Just as Volpone's opening speech on gold calls our attention to those vital natural and social forces which have been perverted by the substitution of a gold coin for the sun, so here our attention is focused on the nature of true medicine, *and true playing,* by the distortion of both those arts wrought by greed and lust, the moving powers behind Scoto-Volpone's performance." But if my reading of the close of the play is correct, Jonson's vision is far more radical. We reject not the abuse of playing but playing itself.

Indeed Scoto's pitch for his worthless snake oil seems to me a brilliant and bitter parody of the central Renaissance defense of the stage. The mountebank tells us that his product is a sovereign cure for all ailments: "the *mal-caduco,* crampes, conuulsions, paralysies, epilepsies, *tremor-cordia,* retyred-nerues, ill vapours of the spleene, stoppings of the liuer, the stone, the strangury, *hernia ventosa, iliaca passio,*" and on and on. We know that the claims are nonsense, but we listen out of sheer delight in the performance itself. The mountebank knows that we know that it is nonsense, but he will never let on, for that would spoil the game and drive away business.

Is this not derisive laughter at those sixteenth- and seventeenth-century apologists for the drama who never tire of telling us that our tuppenny admission is the best investment we could ever make, that plays cure all our moral hernias? Is this not the disturbing self-mockery of the man who in the Dedicatory Epistle to *Volpone* —an epistle addressed to those greatest of gulls, the universities of Oxford and Cambridge—wrote with a straight face of the "impossibility of any mans being the good Poet, without first being a good man"? And the Epistle does not even stop at that extravagant claim for the poet:

> He that is said to be able to informe young-men to all good disciplines, inflame growne-men to all great vertues, keepe oldmen in their best and supreme state, or as they decline to childhood, recouer them to their first strength; that comes forth the interpreter, and arbiter of nature, a teacher of things diuine, no lesse then humane, a master in manners; and can alone (or with a few) effect the businesse of man-kind: this, I take him, is no subiect for pride, and ignorance to exercise their rayling rhetorique vpon.

Now it is clear that Jonson was strongly drawn to these claims, that throughout his career he wanted very much to believe in them. But as a man with a remarkably acute ear for cant and hucksterism, he understood quite well how closely resembled a mountebank's patter.

If there is a convincing defense of the stage in *Volpone,* it is not the pretensions of the humanists but the comically medical promise of the prologue:

All gall, and coppresse, from his inke, he drayneth,
> Onely, a little salt remayneth;
Wherewith, he'll rub your cheeks til (red with laughter)
> They shall looke fresh, a weeke after.

The promise of amusement is recalled at the very close of the play by Volpone himself, who steps forward and speaks directly to the audience:

> The seasoning of a play is the applause.
> Now, though the fox be punish'd by the lawes,
> He, yet, doth hope there is no suffring due,
> For any fact, which he hath done 'gainst you;
> If there be, censure him: here he, doubtfull, stands.
> If not, fare iouially, and clap your hands.

If earlier Volpone seemed like a character who had somehow survived his play, here for a moment he is literally that. And as such he can call attention to the drama as entertainment, hearty fare for which the "seasoning" is applause. A gap is deliberately opened between the play's moral structure—by which Volpone must be punished—and its power to delight. In *The Alchemist* and *Bartholomew Fair,* this gap is exploited to effect a new (if qualified) acceptance of theatricality. But in *Volpone* Jonson has incorporated not only the audience's applause but, as I have suggested, its departure. The exit may be irksome, as Volpone's histrionics are enormously vital and attractive, but as this play bitterly insists, you cannot stay in the theater forever.

Comic Form in Ben Jonson: Volpone and the Philosopher's Stone

Leo Salingar

> *Oh, 'tis imposture all:*
> *And as no chymique yet th' Elixir got,*
>   *But glorifies his pregnant pot,*
>   *If by the way to him befall*
> *Some odoriferous thing, or medicinall,*
>   *So lovers dreame a rich and long delight,*
>   *But get a winter-seeming summers night.*
>   DONNE, "Love's alchymie"

Ben Jonson regularly presented an image of himself, in and beyond his comedies, as a figure of monolithic assurance, consistency and integrity; he could never publicly have agreed with Yeats that a poet makes rhetoric (merely rhetoric) out of his quarrels with others, but poetry out of his quarrels with himself. Behind this image of himself that Jonson projected there were the impulses of an ideal—an ideal both of the Stoic sage, like his own Crites in *Cynthia's Revels* ("humble in his height" but "fixed" and self-sufficient as "a circle bounded in it selfe"), and of the humanistic orator-poet as moral instructor, "the interpreter, and arbiter of nature, . . . a master in manners." Jonson could reply with some justice to his detractors that it was "the offices, and function of a Poet" he was proclaiming, not simply his personal and private merits. But it has always been difficult to distinguish cleanly between learning and pedantry in these proclamations of his, be-

From *English Drama: Forms and Development,* edited by Marie Axton and Raymond Williams. © 1977 by Cambridge University Press.

tween self-assertion and arrogance. Other motives, such as competitiveness, ambition and vanity, seem to be mixed with his affirmation of a noble ideal. Self-advertisement was a professional deformation he shared with other humanists—and charlatans as well—in the world of the Renaissance. And deeper needs to commend himself seem to have been at work. In his anger with the "loathsome" ignorance and "impudence" of his public, there may have been the spark of a suspicion that his own humanism was out-of-date. Worse still, it may have been prompted by the suppressed recognition that his own comedies were not, after all, consistently the best he felt himself capable of. So much, at least, was tactfully hinted by Thomas Carew, the most penetrating of Jonson's "sons," after the older poet's explosion of "immodest rage" over the fiasco of *The New Inn*. Had Jonson's self-approval been as firm and stoical as he professed, he would not have betrayed such an "itch of prayse." He would have acknowledged, without flinching, that

> 'tis true
> Thy comique Muse from the exalted line
> Toucht by thy Alchymist, doth since decline
> From that her Zenith

and he would have carried his laurels with indifference towards "the extorted prayse / Of vulgar breath." In the end, "the quarrell lyes," not with the public, but "Within thyne owne virge."

Drummond of Hawthornden had already drawn, in harsher terms, a similar conclusion about Jonson:

> He is a great lover and praiser of himself, a contemner and Scorner of others, . . . jealous of every word and action of those about him (especiallie after drink, which is one of the Elements in which he liveth), . . . a bragger of some good that he wanteth . . . He is passionately kynde and angry, careless either to gaine or keep . . . : oppressed with fantasie, which hath ever mastered his reason, a generall disease in many poets.

And, if one can attribute something here to the resentment of the provincial host who had been browbeaten by his London guest in his cups, Jonson had evidently provoked the apparently surprising remark about his own oppressive fantasy by such things as his stories of tricking a lady by dressing up as an astrologer, and "consum[ing] a whole night" in contemplation of imaginary battles circling round his great toe. Similarly, fantasy, or poetic "madness," is the theme of the tribute published by James Howell, addressing himself to Jonson as one of his "sons":

> You were madd when you writt your *Fox,* and madder when
> you writt your *Alchymist,* . . . but when you writt your *Epi-*
> *grammes,* and the *Magentic Lady* you were not so madd; Insomuch
> that I perceave ther be degrees of madnes in you; Excuse me
> that I am so free with you. The madnes I meane is that divine
> furie, . . . which *Ovid* speaks of.

Howell and Drummond both agree with each other and with Carew in this, that they see strong impulses in Jonson that are at odds with his public image of himself.

Although Jonson's impatience with "the loathed stage" of his own day never subsided very far below the surface, his confidence in an ideal art of comedy never wavered. Nevertheless, there are differences of emphasis in some of his statements of the ideal, which partly correspond to the differences between his own view of his genius and that of his friends. In his earlier, more propagandist, statements he dwells, as if in assured anticipation, on the effects of comedy, "a thing throughout pleasant, and ridiculous, and accommodated to the correction of manners"; the poet writing comedy "is said to be able to informe yong-men to all good disciplines, inflame growne-men to all great virtues" and even "recover [old-men] to their first strength"—apparently by the sheer force and "justice" of his "doctrine." However, to "sport with humane follies" sounds less peremptory. And in the private notes he put together for *Discoveries,* late in his career, he shifts his attention, though still within the framework of the theory he had always held, from the remote or alleged effects of comedy to the means towards those effects, to what is directly perceived. Of all types of Poet, it is the Comic, he says there, who "comes nearest" that established model of humanist culture, the Ciceronian Orator:

> Because, in moving the minds of men, and stirring of affections
> (in which Oratory shewes, and especially approves her emin-
> ence) hee chiefly excells. What figure of a Body was *Lysippus*
> ever able to forme with his Graver, or *Apelles* to paint with his
> Pencill, as the Comedy to life expresseth so many, and various
> affections of the minde? There shall the Spectator see some,
> insulting with Joy; others, fretting with Melancholy; raging with
> Anger; mad with Love; boiling with Avarice; undone with Riot;
> tortur'd with expectation; consum'd with feare: no perturbation

in common life, but the Orator findes an example of it in the
Scene.

(ll. 2532–43)

The variety and liveliness of the stage, and the "perturbation" of characters
"oppressed with fantasie"—these are the features of comedy that stand out
in Jonson's mind here, rather than the "doctrine" or "justice" of the satirist
behind the scenes. And these, of course, are the features of his own successful
comedies, as distinct from his "dotages" and comparative failures. No doubt
his finest achievements depend at every step on Jonson's rational control,
his unrelaxing pursuit of measure, decorum and justice. But they depend
no less on release of energy from those sources in the poet that Drummond
called fantasy and Howell, madness.

Granting the general bias of Jonson's mind, it seems likely that they
depend even more, as Howell said, on the latter sources. Jonson never
forgets his obligations as a rhetorician, moralist and contriver of intrigues
in his comedies. But in half of them, his machinery is too ponderous for
his material; he takes himself too seriously; there is no proportion between
the intellectual power exerted and the triviality or the merely schematic
significance of the characters. *Every Man in His Humour* is an exception,
but there Jonson is altogether unusually lighthearted. We only see him at
his full stretch in his comedies of sustained "perturbation," in *Volpone, The
Silent Woman, The Alchemist* and *Bartholomew Fair*. And even among those,
there is surely a distinction between the two prose works and his two
generally acknowledged masterpieces. *The Silent Woman* and *Bartholomew
Fair* have a crowded vigour that no other English dramatist, I believe, can
match, but even so, they remain top-heavy because the comic butts are too
cramped, too limited to repay the full benefit of Jonson's laughter at their
expense; he presents them as eccentrics rather than types. What distinguishes
Volpone and *The Alchemist* is not simply the resonance and mock-heroic
grandeur of Jonson's verse, but the generality of their comic themes. Their
people can still be described as caricatures, but they are caricatures of deep-
rooted human impulses, which seem universal even in the distorted form
that Jonson imposes on them. Indeed, the distortion is necessary to the
impression of universality, since it develops in each play from a common
imaginative centre, with the result that the characters reinforce one another,
with all their variations and extensions of gullibility and greed.

I want to suggest that there is essentially one theme at the centre of
both plays, namely the idea of alchemy, or what Jonson found in it; to
borrow the term Mr Ray Heffner has applied to *The Silent Woman* and

Bartholomew Fair, alchemy is the "unifying symbol" in *Volpone,* where it is latent, as well as in the companion masterpiece, where it is declared. Whatever psychological causes may have favoured the choice, this theme gave Jonson the release he apparently needed for both sides of his personality at once, the rational and the fantastic, more than any other theme in his comic repertory. For one thing, the hope of converting base metals to gold epitomised the acquistiveness that Jonson saw as both a permanent human failing and the special driving force in his own world, in an age of mercantilism, inflation, and social pushing. Secondly, the hope of finding in the philosopher's stone an elixir of life, a panacea for all diseases and sort of hormone-substitute to confer prolonged vitality, represented a clinging to life even more primitive and deep-seated than the desire for easy money; it is the force of this motif that makes one of the principal differences between *Volpone* and *The Alchemist* on one side, and on the other, *The Devil Is an Ass* and *The Staple of News,* where Jonson's allegory is more barely economic. And alchemy, which was particularly flourishing in the century after Paracelsus, offered not merely a fertile ground for quackery and delusion, as Chaucer and Erasmus had shown, but a satirically attractive pseudo-religion, with its overtones of occult theosophy and its carapace of jargon. Because of its pretensions as a philosophy of nature and an esoteric tradition, it provided Jonson with the most general symbol he could probably have found for the self-willed shams he wanted to attack in the learning, religion and social behaviour around him—more general, certainly, in its intellectual applications, than puritanism or the ballyhoo of the marketplace or the humours of gentility. It was a supremely typical example of fantasy in thought and action. Treated as a "unifying symbol," alchemy fitted in with Jonson's admiration for the classical satirists and for the humanism of More and Erasmus; at the same time, it enabled him to carry further his ambition to adapt some of the basic forms of Old Comedy to the Elizabethan stage. He made of it the image of a latter-day world-upside-down, a counter-Utopia.

Like other Elizabethans, Jonson learned much of his art in comedy from Plautus and Terence and their Italian followers. And he paid much more attention than his rivals to Renaissance theory, including the principle of concentration of interest implied in the unities of time and place, and the principle of calculated progress towards a climax implied in the parallel between plays and orations. His "art," as he says, "appears most full of lustre" when his humourists are "laid flat" just as they have reached their "flame and height"; he puts his comic intrigues together like the parts of a "clock," so that all the pieces interact, but the "catastrophe" is delayed or "perplexed," "till some unexpected and new encounter breake out to rectifie all, and make good the *Conclusion*." At the same time, Jonson develops his own distinctive method of construction, whereby he sets going a number of interests or intrigues that are separate at first, but are drawn together and inter-involved, like the currents in a whirlpool, at significant centres of action (such as Paul's Walk and then Saviolina's apartment at court in *Every Man out of His Humour,* or the pig-woman's booth and then the puppet-show in *Bartholomew Fair*). This is one of the main resources behind his crescendo effects.

Insofar as Jonson drew his separate characters together by the allurements of a common folly or vice, he was plainly following the example of the Tudor moralities. But the principal stimulus behind his methods of construction must have been the example of Aristophanes (in whom the art of comedy "appeared absolute, and fully perfected," in spite of his "scurrility"). Aristophanes provided Jonson not only with precedents for topical satire including instruction and horseplay and "a mingling of fantasy and realism," but suggestive examples of "a comic structure centered . . . on the exploration of an extravagant conceit." The typical ground plan of an Aristophanic comedy could be described as the execution of a preposterous scheme which brings characters of all sorts flocking round its originator. So, in *Plutus,* for example, the neighbours flock to Chremylus's house as soon as it is known that he is lodging the Wealth-god there after hitting on the idea of curing the god of his blindness—and not only the neighbours, but a host of strangers, a Just Man, an Informer, an Old Woman who has lost her kept lover, the Youth in question, Hermes (the jack-of-all-trades among the gods), the Priest of Zeus, and even Zeus the Preserver himself. So, similarly, people flock to a common attraction in *Volpone* and *The Alchemist,* and Volpone can boast that his reputation

> drawes new clients, daily, to my house,
> Women, and men, of every sexe, and age.
> (1.1.76)

And they flock for comparable reasons: Aristophanes' account of Plutus (who is not only blind at first, but does not know his own powers) is the prime literary source for the god that Volpone and his "clients" worship,

> Riches, the dumbe god, that giv'st all men tongues:
> That canst doe nought, and yet mak'st men doe all things.
> (1.1.22)

Both dramatists build on similar premises. It is true that Aristophanes has been given a variety of interpretations. And his comedies expound Utopian schemes, patently fabulous, though allegedly beneficial; whereas the schemes Jonson invents for his ticksters are plausible, but fraudulent. The "extravagant conceit" that Aristophanes develops in *Plutus* and his earlier plays involves that poetic fiction of restoring Athens to a golden age, whereas the talk of a golden age in *Volpone* and *The Alchemist* is an impudent cheat. Nevertheless, Jonson's debt to the Greek poet is vital, in that he constructs his plays around a fantastic project that overturns the values publicly honoured by society, a project that is alluring precisely because it is outrageous and defies the limits of nature. The sexual licence and the dream of rejuvenation or perpetual vigour that Jonson associates with the golden metal in *Volpone* and *The Alchemist* also belong to the scheme of things in Aristophanes.

Though *Plutus* has lost rank with modern students of Aristophanes, it was the favourite among his comedies with Jonson's age. And, for Jonson, the critique of money it contains was reinforced by later classical satirists, particularly Lucian, whose "mery conceytes and jestes" had already "delyted" the wise Utopians. Lucian's *Dialogues of the Dead,* some of which Erasmus had translated, are prominent among the sources commonly cited for the plot of legacy-hunting in *Volpone.* Even more important in this connection, I think, was Lucian's *Timon,* which Erasmus had also translated. In this semi-dramatic dialogue, which darts across Lucian's characteristic satiric themes of mythology, superstition and philosophical imposture, the principal topic, following Aristophanes' *Plutus,* is the inequality and instability of wealth, and its moral consequences. Timon clamours to Zeus because in his poverty he is ignored by the very men he had flooded with gifts when rich; Zeus at last deigns to listen, and sends Plutus with Hermes down to him with a gift of treasure; whereupon Timon hugs his lucky gold to himself—and beats off the train of sycophants who have immediately hurried to renew his friendship. A cluster of details from the dialogue reappear in *Volpone.* For instance, Hermes points out to Zeus the advantages of shouting loudly (like Voltore) when pleading in court; Zeus refers to the type of a miser, defrauded by "a cursed valet or a shackle-burnishing steward," like Mosca ("*aut sceleratissimus famulus, aut dispensator*"); Plutus compares some of the misusers of wealth to a man who (like Corvino) "should take a young and beautiful woman for his lawful wife" and should then "himself induce her to commit adultery." In the manner of the *Dialogues of the Dead,* Plutus also sketches the case of legacy-hunters who find that all their "bait," their expectant gifts, have been wasted when the will is published, while the estate may pass to some "toady or lewd slave" (like Mosca, again) who promptly gives himself airs, changes his name, and "insults gentlemen," before squandering his gains on flatterers in his turn. Those who "gape" after money are not necessarily blind, Plutus explains, but have their vision darkened by "Ignorance and Deceit, who now hold sway everywhere." They are repeatedly compared to birds and beasts; for instance, Hermes calls Timon's hangers-on during his first prosperity so many "ravens and wolves" and "birds of prey" (*corvi, lupi, vultures*). Here Jonson could have found the principal suggestion for his animal fable and the names of his Venetians.

Moreover, Timon's reaction when he strikes treasure with his pick foreshadows the ethic that Volpone is to live by:

> O Hermes, god of gain! Where did all this gold come from? Is this a dream? I am afraid I may wake up and find nothing but ashes. No, . . . it is coined gold. . . .
> "O gold, thou fairest gift that comes to man!"
> In very truth you stand out like blazing fire, not only by night but by day. . . . Now I am convinced that Zeus once turned into gold, for what maid would open her bosom and receive so beautiful a lover?

He resolves to build a tower for himself alone over the treasure, where he intends to be buried; and he promulgates for himself a law of egoism:

> "Be it resolved and enacted into law, . . . that I shall associate with no one, recognise no one and scorn everyone. Friends, guests, comrades and Altars of Mercy shall be matters for boundless mockery. To pity one who weeps, to help one who is in need shall be a misdemeanour and an infringement of the constitution [*morum subversio*]. My life shall be solitary, like that of wolves; Timon shall be my only friend, and all others shall be enemies and conspirators. . . . Tribe, clan, deme and native land itself shall be inane and useless names, and objects of the zeal of fools. Timon shall keep his wealth to himself, scorn everyone and live in luxury all by himself, remote from flattery and tiresome praise. . . . Be it once for all resolved that he shall give himself the farewell handclasp when he comes to die, and shall set the funeral wreath on his own brow."

Volpone's tactics, of course, are to be directly opposite; he is to be a fox, not a wolf. But his egoism is a variant of Timon's misanthropy. When he opens his "shrine" in the first scene, he too hails his gold "like a flame, by night; or like the day / Strooke out of *chaos*"; he too adorns it with poetic fables, as "the best of things: and far transcending / All stile"—"inane and useless names"—"of joy in children, parents, friends." For him, as for Timon, the very idea of commiseration for others becomes a subject for scorn, as in the flattery he laps up from Mosca:

> You lothe, the widdowes, or the orphans teares
> Should wash your pavements; or their pittious cryes
> Ring in your roofes.

His basic motive for alluring clients instead of beating them off is the same as Timon's:

> What should I doe,
> But cocker up my *genius,* and live free
> To all delights, my fortune calls me to?
> I have no wife, no parent, child, allie,
> To give my substance to; but whom I make
> Must be my heire: and this makes men observe me.

And even his final and fatal trick of tormenting his dupes by spreading in person the rumour of his own death keeps in line with Timon's earnest wish to be chief if not sole mourner at his own funeral. In short, it appears as if Jonson, while inverting the circumstances, has taken over the moral scheme of Lucian's satire. Conceivably—to go a step further—it was Jonson who aroused Shakespeare's interest in *Timon.*

His debt to Lucian did not end with the legacy-hunting plot. The grotesque interlude Mosca has devised for Volpone's private delectation is taken (with reinforcements out of *The Praise of Folly*) from Lucian's dialogue of *The Dream, or The Cock,* which again combines economic and philosophical satire, this time emphasising the Pythagorean doctrine of the transmigration of souls. And, as Harry Levin has claimed, the notion of metempsychosis goes "to the core" of *Volpone* and of much in Jonson's later writing. It stands for much more than a philosophical fantasy. On one side, Jonson makes it analogous to the transformation of substances in alchemy. On the other side, he relates the notion of shifting and transformed identities to the theatrical business of disguise or deception, to the principle of acting a part.

When Marlowe makes Barabas boast of his enormous profits, "Infinite riches in a little roome," his language is arrogant and highly coloured, but there is nothing bizarre or mysterious about it; the merchant is simply a sharp operator exploiting favourable conditions. Volpone's attitude towards his gold is decidedly more complex. He too is clearly intended to dominate the world of the play in and by fulfilling that "desire of gold" whose compulsion most of those around him are too hypocritical to acknowledge. But it is also clear from the outset that neither Volpone nor his creator is to be satisfied with that dramatic function alone. From Volpone's first lines to his hoard, "my *saint*," "the worlds soule, and mine," it becomes clear that he is not content merely with beating the rest of the world at their own game, but sees himself as the discoverer of a truly human destiny, which other men in their vanity have been simply blind to; he is full of scorn at their expense, but he does not adopt the pose of a disillusioned cynic. On the contrary, he sounds more like a man with a revelation, an enthusiast. According to C. H. Herford, his opening speech is a "hymn" which "transfigures avarice with the glamour of religion and idealism." To this comment, L. C. Knights has objected that it omits the essential, Jonson's irony; the speech "brings the popular and religious tradition into play, but that is a different matter; religion and the riches of the teeming earth are there for the purpose of ironic contrast." But this, in turn, understates Jonson's scope and resourcefulness in his rhetoric.

No doubt Volpone brands himself with egregious folly when he speaks of his gold "darkening" the sun and "far transcending" love or companionship; with perversity, when he exclaims,

> Well did wise Poets, by thy glorious name,
> Title that age, which they would have the best

and with grovelling superstition, when he repeats the word, "saint," and offers to

> kisse
> With adoration, thee, and every relique
> Of sacred treasure, in this blessed roome.

Nevertheless, "popular and religious tradition" would hardly dispose of him automatically for a Jacobean (not to speak of a modern) audience. When, for instance, in line 3 he hails gold as the world's "soule," is he a sophist—or perhaps a mystic? There is awe, as well as impish belittlement, in his image of "the teeming earth" beholding "the long'd-for sunne / Peepe through the hornes of the celestiall *ram*"; and his awe takes on a biblical splendour when (in the image probably suggested by Lucian's Timon) he compares his gold not only to "a flame, by night" but to

> the day
> Strooke out of *chaos*, when all darkenesse fled
> Unto the center.

For his next epithet, "O, thou son of SOL," Volpone borrows the language of alchemy; and even though Jonson diverts the effect at once towards anti-climax—with "(But brighter then thy father)"—some hint remains of a mystical faith of system at work behind the speaker's rhapsody. While an audience can be sure that Volpone's mythology is false, they are not likely to be supplied with a prompt retort from tradition; surely "wise Poets," purveyors of secrets as they were, must have had some arcane reason for giving the "glorious name" of golden to the "best" of ages? There is a similar hint of clairvoyance within his impudence when Volpone makes gold "far transcend" human love—the vain "stile" of it,—"Or any other waking dreame on earth." As he works towards a climax, our confident suspicion that nevertheless he has merely been juggling with paradox is brought crashing against the gross facts of common experience (or common opinion) about the power of money:

> That canst doe nought, and yet mak'st men doe all things;
> The price of soules; even hell, with thee to boot,
> Is made worth heaven! Thou art vertue, fame,
> Honour, and all things else!

And even though Mosca is allowed to deflate his patron by means of an equivocal assent—

> Riches are in fortune
> A greater good, then wisedome is in nature—

Volpone has still a higher card in his hand:

> Yet, I glory
> More in the cunning purchase of my wealth,
> Then in the glad possession; since I gaine
> No common way.

He is not, like Barabas, simply first among equals, but belongs to a different order of being; beside his cult of gain, the usual avenues to profit are destructive as well as trivial, so that "nature" appears to be on his side, in addition to "fortune":

> I use no trade, no venter;
> I wound no earth with plow-shares; fat no beasts
> To feede the shambles; have no mills for yron,
> Oyle, corne, or men, to grinde 'hem into poulder;

> I blow no subtill glasse; expose no ships
> To threatnings of the furrow-faced sea;
> I turne no moneys, in the publike banke;
> Nor usure private.

On returning from Utopia, Raphael Hythlodaye had perceived in the so-called "commen wealth" at home nothing better than "a certein conspiracy of riche men," stained with "fraud, theft, ravine" and yet undermined with "feare, griefe, care, laboures and watchinges"; Volpone has blandly appropriated some of this stern radicalism, combining it with a solicitous concern for Nature. And though we may feel positive already that he is practising some confidence trick, we have not been told yet what his "cunning purchase" is. Our first general impression of him includes an uneasy perception that he is something more esoteric than a superlative swindler. Mystification is part of his character.

Volpone speaks like a virtuoso or an artist, in the special Renaissance sense of one initiated into Nature's secrets. He does not practise alchemy (he need not take the trouble), but he both nourishes and feeds upon the same extravagant hopes. According, for example, to Cornelius Agrippa—writing for the time being as an authoritative critic, with inside knowledge,—it is doubtful whether alchemy should really "be termed an Arte, or a counterfaite colouring, or a pursuite of nature," but in any case it is certainly "a notable and a suffered deceipte":

> The vanity whereof is easily perceyved in this, that it promiseth the thinges whiche nature in no wise can abide, nor attaine, whereas no Arte can surmounte nature, but doth imitate, and folowe it aloofe of [f], and the force of nature is farre stronger than of Arte. . . . Whilst that they go about to alter the kinds of thinges, and suppose to forge (as they say) a certaine blissed stone of Philosophers, with the which like *Midas,* all bodies touched become golde and silver: moreover they endeavoure to make a certaine *Quint essence* to come down from the high and inaccessible heaven, by the means whereof they promise us not onely more riches than *Croesus* had, but also expelling olde age, do promise us youth and continuall health, and almost immortalitie togither with great substance.
> (Henry Cornelius Agrippa, *Of the Vanitie and uncertaintie of Artes and Sciences)*

Such fallacies are smiled at in Volpone's Venice, as when Mosca greets Corbaccio, carrying his "bag of bright *cecchines*":

> This is true physick, this your sacred medicine,
> No talke of *opiates,* to this great *elixir.*
>
> (1.4.69)

But Corbaccio is goaded by precisely the delusions that alchemy fosters, as Volpone proclaims the moment his doddering visitant has left:

> So many cares, so many maladies,
> So many fears attending on old age,
> Yea, death so often call'd on, as no wish
> Can be more frequent with 'hem, their limbs faint,
> Their senses dull, their seeing, hearing, going,
> All dead before them; yea, their very teeth,
> Their instruments of eating, fayling them:
> Yet this is reckon'd life! Nay, here was one,
> Is now gone home, that wishes to live longer!
> Feeles not his gout, nor palsie, faines himselfe
> Yonger, by scores of yeeres, flatters his age,
> With confident belying it, hopes he may
> With charmes, like AESON, have his youth restor'd:
> And with these thoughts so battens, as if fate
> Would be as easily cheated on, as he,
> And all turnes aire!
>
> (1.4.144)

Volpone mocks Corbaccio as if the old man believed literally in the myths of rejuvenation from Aristophanes, and he draws a conclusion exactly parallel to the fate in store for Subtle and his companions: "Selling of flyes, flat bawdry, with the *stone:* / Till it, and they, and all in *fume* are gone." Volpone speaks with a crushing sense of physical reality, with the weight of a long-tested moral tradition behind his words.

But the very tautness of Volpone's irony here demonstrates the pull of the opposing illusion. And Volpone himself is a kind of quintessence extracted from the vices of his clients, greed, double-dealing, loquacity and perversion. When he diagnoses Corbaccio's folly, he has already been heard responding to a piece of flattery from Mosca that could have been taken from the *Dialogues of the Dead*:

> when I am lost in blended dust,
> And hundred such, as I am, in succession—
> —Nay, that were too much, MOSCA.—You shall live,
> Still, to delude these *harpyies.*—Loving MOSCA.
>
> (1.2.119)

And the whole of his "cunning purchase" depends, of course, on shamming
the condition of men like Corbaccio, with

> my fain'd cough, my phthisick, and my gout,
> My apoplexie, palsie, and catarrhes.
>
> (1.2.124)

So that when he jumps from his pretended sickbed to ridicule Corbaccio,
Volpone is tacitly acting for his own benefit the illusion he professes to
pierce in others.

The sense that Volpone pursues an elixir, or believes he already pos-
sesses an equally magical secret, is all the more potent in the play because
his obsession is not directly named. Not to say what he is after is part of
his mystification; and, if anything, he thinks of himself as a Machiavellian,
rather than a vulgar adept; (part of the effect of Sir Pol's role in the comedy
is to throw light on this kind of self-deception among the Venetians). But
Volpone is an adept in spite of himself. As soon as his imagination has been
inflamed by the mere description of Celia, the course he takes to see her is
to disguise himself as a mountebank, with a "precious liquor" for sale:

> O, health! health! the blessing of the rich! the riches of the poore!
> who can buy thee at too deare a rate, since there is no enjoying
> this world, without thee? Be not then so sparing of your purses,
> honorable gentlemen, as to abridge the naturall course of life
> . . . For, when a humide fluxe, or catarrhe, by the mutability
> of aire, falls from your head, into an arme, or shoulder, or any
> other part; take you a duckat, or your *cecchine* of gold, and apply
> to the place affected: see, what good effect it can worke. No,
> no, 'tis this blessed *unguento,* this rare extraction, that hath only
> power to disperse all malignant humours.
>
> (2.2.84)

And, once he has caught Celia's attention from her window, he tries to
hold it with praise of an even rarer secret, his powder

> of which, if I should speake to the worth, nine thousand volumes
> were but as one page, that page as a line, that line as a word: so
> short is this pilgrimage of man (which some call life) to the
> expressing of it. . . . It is the poulder, that made VENUS a
> goddesse (given her by APOLLO) that kept her perpetually
> young, clear'd her wrincles, firm'd her gummes, fill'd her skin,
> colour'd her hair; . . . where ever it but touches, in youth it

perpetually preserves, in age restores the complexion; seat's your
teeth, did they dance like virginall jacks, firme as a wall.

(2.2.228)

Volpone here is acting, but acting with conviction; he is not trying simply
to deceive the ignorant crowd, but to make an impression on the woman
he intends to seduce. His rhapsody of perpetual "life" is an ironic sequel
to his diagnosis of Corbaccio.

Similarly, when he tries to seduce Celia, it is the dream of sexual vigour
perpetually renewed that animates him, as he throws off his disguise of
decrepit age:

> I am, now, as fresh,
> As hot, as high, and in a joviall plight,
> As when (in that so celebrated *scene,*
> At recitation of our *comœdie,*
> For entertainement of the great VALOYS)
> I acted yong ANTINOUS.

(3.7.157)

A Jacobean spectator, struck by the precise reference, could have reflected
that the role had been hardly flattering to the actor's virility, and that the
famous "entertainement" was some thirty years back. In any case, the
present Volpone must be old enough for the rumour of his physical decay
to be believed. Yet what riles him, when Celia holds him off, is the horror
reflected in his own lucrative pretence:

> Thinke me cold,
> Frosen, and impotent, and so report me?
> That I had NESTOR's *hernia,* thou wouldst thinke.

(3.7.260)

It is significant that the turning-point of the play should come here, in a
scene of attempted rape, and not in an episode of fraud. References to health,
medicine, disease, images connected with the life-force, are even more
insistent than thoughts and images connected with money. And with an
exact sense of the appropriate, Jonson has Volpone sentenced at the end,
not for obtaining money under false pretences but for simulating disease:

> our judgement on thee
> Is, that thy substance all be straight confiscate
> To the hospitall, of the *Incurabili:*
> And, since the most was gotten by imposture,

By faining lame, gout, palsey, and such diseases,
Thou art to lie in prison, crampt with irons,
Till thou bee'st sicke, and lame indeed.

(5.12.118)

Volpone has been "by bloud, and ranke a gentleman," stooping to a beggar's cony-catching tricks. But his essential crime has been an offence against Nature.

When Shakespeare discusses drama, in *Hamlet*, for instance, his mind is chiefly on the actor; when Jonson discusses it, in his many prologues and interscenes, he is concerned with the poet. In Shakespeare's comedies, disguise, or play-acting within the play, usually creates a beneficial illusion; in Jonson, it usually expresses imposture, and the removal of a disguise is the exposure of a sham. He is altogether more aloof towards the players than his rival. Nevertheless, he must have observed the technique of acting very closely, and the thought of acting stood for something influential in his general view of life. "I have considered," he was to write in *Discoveries,*

Our whole life is like a *Play*: wherein every man, forgetfull of himselfe, is in travaile with expression of another. Nay, wee so insist in imitating others, as wee cannot (when it is necessary) returne to our selves: like Children, that imitate the vices of *Stammerers* so long, till at last they become such; and make the habit to another nature, as it is never forgotten.

(ll. 1093–99)

The comparison of life to a play was of course a Renaissance commonplace, but Jonson's particular application of it here was unusual, if not unique. It contrasts sharply with his public image of himself. It suggests that there were motives arising from self-inspection and self-protection behind his repeated attacks on "humours," charlatanism and social apery.

Volpone expresses this side of Jonson's vision of life more completely than any other of his characters. Materially speaking, the magnifico does not need to go in for fraud. He does it for his private "glory," to "cocker up [his] *genius*"; he feels a compulsion towards play-acting, preferably with a strain of the abnormal or the exotic. He needs spectators, but secret spectators whom he governs, including "the curious" and "the envious," whom he imagines spying on his love-making with Celia (3.7.236–39). Above all, he needs to act a part, to the accompaniment of his own applause. A man of mature age, he feigns senility. As a would-be love-adventurer, he mimics a charlatan. Having recalled, to impress Celia, an image of himself as a youthful actor, he tries to dazzle her, beyond the pitch of "*vertigo*," with the prospect of making love "in changed shapes," copied from Ovid's *Metamorphoses* and then furnished from a collector's wardrobe of exotic "moderne formes" (3.7.219, 221–55). Finally, escaping, thanks to Mosca, from the fear of exposure, his immediate recoil is to look for "Any device, now, of rare, ingenious knavery, / That would possesse me with a violent laughter" (5.1.14), so that he brings retribution down on himself by way of his superfluous disguise as an officer of the law. Jonson has calculated Volpone's assumed roles so as to reflect back on his real personality; or rather, to reflect back on a being with a compulsive ego but no firm identity, a man perpetually "forgetfull of himselfe" and "in travaile with expression of another."

In this respect, Volpone is by no means alone in the play. Except for Celia and Bonario, who necessary symbols rather than characters, all the people of the play, English as well as Venetian, are engaged in pretences, stratagems real or imaginary, or sudden and opportunist changes of front. Even the court of law, at the end, is not exempt. Indeed, the theme of systematic insincerity is first put clearly into words with regard to the lawyer, Voltore, when Mosca flatters his hopes of inheriting Volpone's fortune:

> He ever lik'd your course, sir, that first tooke him.
> I, oft, have heard him say, how he admir'd
> Men of your large profession, that could speake
> To every cause, and that mere contraries,
> Till they were hoarse againe, yet all be law.
>
> (1.3.51)

The ironies of the word "profession" are carried over from *The Few of Malta,* but Mosca develops them with a zest of his own:

> That, with most quick agilitie, could turne,
> And re-turne; make knots, and undoe them;
> Give forked counsell; take provoking gold
> On either hand, and put it up: these men,
> He knew, would thrive, with their humilitie.

And it is fitting that this cinematograph of the hypocrite in motion should come from Mosca, the Fly, the mobile demon of equivocation. When (developing a theme possibly suggested by one of the dialogues under Lucian's name) Mosca dilates on the praise of his own life-style, it is the physical, existential qualities of the affair that receive his fondest attention:

> I feare, I shall begin to grow in love
> With my deare selfe, and my most prosp'rous parts,
> They doe so spring, and burgeon; I can feele
> A whimsey i' my bloud: (I know not how)
> Successe hath made me wanton.

(3.1.1)

He feels a biological transformation:

>   I could skip
>   Out of my skin, now, like a subtill snake,
>   I am so limber.

And, for Mosca, it is precisely versatility, changefulness, that distinguishes "your Parasite" in the scale of creation:

>   All the wise world is little else, in nature,
>   But Parasites, or Sub-parasites.

The parasite's "mystery" is "a most precious thing, dropt from above"; by rights, a liberal "science":

>   And, yet,
>   I meane not those, that have your bare towne-arte,
>   To know, who's fit to feede 'hem;

nor does he mean those with a merely animal flexibility:

>   With their court-dog-tricks, that can fawne, and fleere,
>   Make their revenue out of legs, and faces,
>   Eccho my-Lord, and lick away a moath.

No, Mosca's true-born parasite is a "sparke" so volatile that he has no position in space or discernible identity at all:

>   your fine, elegant rascall, that can rise,
>   And stoope (almost together) like an arrow;
>   Shoot through the aire, as nimbly as a starre;
>   Turne short, as doth a swallow; and be here,
>   And there, and here, and yonder, all at once;
>   Present to any humour, all occasion;
>   And change a visor, swifter, then a thought!

Puck or Ariel could not do better. Poetically, Mosca deserves to outmanoeuvre his patron; he does not act metamorphoses, metamorphoses are the element he lives in.

Jonson restates the principles Mosca stands for in *The Alchemist*, with fresh embellishments of burlesque: for instance, in the scene (2.5) where Subtle calls on the well-schooled Face to recite "the vexations, and the martyrizations / Of metalls, in the worke," and to "answere" Ananias, "i' the language":

> S:—Your *magisterium,* now?
> What's that? F:—Shifting, sir, your elements,
> Drie into cold, cold into moist, moist in—
> to hot, hot into drie. S:—This's *heathen Greeke* to you, still?
> Your *lapis philosophicus?* F:—'Tis a stone, and not
> A *stone; a spirit, a soule, and a body:*
> Which, if you doe *dissolve,* it is *dissolv'd,*
> If you *coagulate,* it is *coagulated,*
> If you make it to *flye,* it *flyeth.*
>
> (ll. 36–44)

In this brilliant parody, which reproduces the technicalities of the Hermetic art with a minimum of distortion, Jonson incidentally defines the speaker's role as well. Face is like the claims for the philosopher's stone because he can be almost anything or everything at once—which means that (until he declines again to Jeremy, the butler) he is really nothing at all, or an actor's mask. He embodies Mosca's philosophy of metempsychosis, of the being that is a nonbeing because it is incessantly something else; and for this dramatic purpose, his connection with alchemy supplies no more than a habitation and a name. But the dramatist had already seized on the connection in *Volpone,* and had sketched it in with reference to Mosca himself. When Mosca and Volpone are gloating over their successful imposture at the first trial, and are planning already to "vexe" the dupes further with Volpone's new—and reckless—"device," Mosca introduces the metaphor of alchemy, with his customary ironic reservations, and Volpone, self-blinded, carries the metaphor on:

> M:—. . . My Lady too, that came into the court,
> To beare false witnesse, for your worship—V:—Yes,
> And kist mee 'fore the fathers; when my face
> Flow'd all with oyles. M:—And sweate, sir. Why, your gold
> Is such another med'cine, it dries up
> All those offensive savors! It transformes
> The most deformed, and restores 'hem lovely,
> As 'twere the strange poeticall girdle. JOVE
> Could no invent, t'himselfe, a shroud more subtile,

> To passe A CRISIUS guardes. It is the thing
> Makes all the world her grace, her youth, her beauty.
>
> . . . .
>
> V: —I'le to my place,
> Thou, to thy posture. M:—I am set. V:—But, MOSCA,
> Play the artificer now, torture 'hem, rarely.
>
> (5.2.95–111)

Already, by metaphor, Jonson has given Mosca the tasks of "vexing" and "torturing" metals that he was later to assign to Face. And the qualities Jonson finds in Mosca's metaphor are the essential poetic characteristics of the play as a whole—animal, mineral and vegetable properties "transformed" into one another, emotional and moral values rendered "false" in the utterance, poetic hyperbole gilding deceit.

In a world where hardly anyone follows fixed principles, nearly anything can happen, as the rogues in *Volpone* find to their cost: Corvino rushes his wife into the trap "too soone" for Mosca's plans (3.7.1), Mosca snatches too eagerly at Volpone's last deception. Jonson constructs his play by making the compulsive fantasies in his characters collide with one another in a "vertigo," in a dizzying spiral. He repeats this method, with even greater virtuosity, in the action of *The Alchemist*. The rogues there manipulate their dupes as before, Sir Epicure's dream of endless vigour in an age of gold is much the same as Volpone's, the intrigue shifts, as before, from money to sex. The dupes in *The Alchemist* are more numerous and varied. And, with "the language" to support him, Jonson deploys his rhetoric in a bacchic extravaganza of impostures of speech—technical jargon, varieties of London slang, Spanish, fairy vocables, Puritan cant, theosophical claptrap—until meaning itself (in Dol's assumed frenzy) threatens to disintegrate, like the materials submitted to Subtle's furnace, into

> *the antient us'd communion*
> *Of vowells, and consonants—. . .*
> *A wisedome, which PYTHAGORAS held most high.*
>
> (4.5.19)

But although *The Alchemist* gives a further range to Jonson's command of rhetoric, he had already prepared for it in *Volpone*. He had already discovered there the poetic value for him of the idea of alchemy, as a latent symbol unifying mystification and power-fantasies with images of "Pythagorean" transformations and comic myths adapted from Aristophanes and Lucian. In several of his masques he returns to the same complex of themes—the revival of Nature, "that impostor Plutus" impersonating Cupid, and alchemy as the rival of genuine art and learning.

Though alchemy was a controversial subject when Jonson was writing, the theory enjoyed exceptional prestige, even (or especially) among scientists. Jonson must have owed the spirit, though not the details, of his own critique largely to Bacon, whom he praises, in *Discoveries,* more unreservedly than any other contemporary. And it also seems possible that he owed the crystallising touch in *Volpone* to *The Advancement of Learning,* which he could have read in 1605, just before the rapid composition of the play. Years later, in *Discoveries,* Jonson summarised a section of the *Advancement,* following Bacon's words closely, in the course of a discussion (ll. 2031–224) of a question vital to the poet, speech as an image of the mind:

> It was well noted by the late L. St. *Alban,* that the study of words is the first distemper of Learning: Vaine matter the second: And a third distemper is deceit, or the likenesse of truth; Imposture held up by credulity.
>
> (ll. 2090–93)

In Bacon's words, deceit is the "foulest" disease of learning,

> as that which doth destroy the essential form of knowledge, which is nothing but a representation of truth: for the truth of being and the truth of knowing are one, differing no more than the direct beam and the beam reflected.

This conjunction of knowledge and reality, and hence of learning and life, evidently impressed the dramatist deeply; and Bacon continues by defining, in effect, the psychological laws of Volpone's world—even providing a theoretical justification for the introduction of the prattling Sir Pol and Lady Would-be, to mimic the Venetians:

> This vice therefore brancheth itself into two sorts; delight in deceiving, and aptness to be deceived; imposture and credulity; which, although they appear to be of a diverse nature, the one seeming to proceed of cunning, and the other of simplicity, yet certainly they do for the most part concur: for as . . . an inquisitive man is a prattler, so upon the like reason a credulous man is a deceiver.

And finally, Bacon lists alchemy among the "arts" or "sciences" most productive of deceit "for the facility of credit which is yielded" to them:

> The sciences themselves which have had better intelligence and confederacy with the imagination of man than with his reason,

are three in number; Astrology, Natural Magic, and Alchemy; of which sciences nevertheless the ends or pretences are noble. For . . . alchemy pretendeth to make separation of all the unlike parts of bodies which in mixtures of nature are incorporate. But the derivations and prosecutions to these ends, both in the theories and in the practices, are full of error and vanity; which the great professors themselves have sought to veil over and conceal by enigmatical writings, and referring themselves to auricular traditions, and such other devices to save the credit of impostures.

In this section, which Jonson summarised as a whole, Bacon was not dealing with any picturesque illustration for argument's sake, or any freakish sideline, but with a major entanglement of contemporary thought. For Bacon, the section contained the germs of his subsequent aphorisms on the Idols of the Mind. For Jonson, it seems hardly too much to say, it contained the germs of both *Volpone* and *The Alchemist*.

Bacon has reservations, particularly in favour of alchemy. He does not reject the claims for it outright, and there was no sufficient reason in the science of the period why he should. Nor does Jonson show that he rejects them completely. On the contrary, he makes Subtle draw more varied customers, and arouse more varied feelings, than the cheats and visionaries satirised by Chaucer or Erasmus; and he could hardly have thrown so much force of mind into the play if he had assumed that Subtle's art stood for no more than a transparent fraud or a hopelessly discredited fallacy. Bacon had said that "confederacy with the imagination" was the source of deceit in alchemy, not ignorance or blatant falsehood; and Jonson's attitude towards the theory of the subject seems like an unwilling suspension of disbelief. He could not have brought so much life into the organisation of *The Alchemist,* or of *Volpone,* if his attitude towards the idea at the centre of both plays had been remote, and single-minded.

Comic Language in *Volpone*

L. A. Beaurline

Ben Jonson was especially skillful in his verbal repetitions, and his work offers many illustration of their possibilities. Jonson exploits them to such an extent that speeches often seem prolix to readers, yet they are economical in their dramatic uses. Only a few examples are necessary to suggest their pervasiveness. Corbaccio repeatedly mishears Mosca's remarks about "dying" Volpone, and Corbaccio's all-consuming fears condition his responses—"What mends he?" "Not I his heir?" "How, how? stronger than he was wont?" (*Volpone*, 1.4). Kastril repeatedly uses terms from quarreling, even when he is ignorant of their meaning (*Alchemist*, 4.7). Morose repeats orders to his servant—"Answer me not by speech but by silence, unless it be otherwise." Morose's constant, overblown exclamations are roared at the audience: "Oh! what villain! What prodigy of mankind is that?" "Oh, shut the door, shut the door." (*Epicoene*, 2.2). Justice Overdo reiterates his judgments of the "enormities" at Bartholomew Fair, as relentlessly as any outraged judge in a Victorian farce. To the end of his career, Jonson exploited opportunities for comic repetition, and his use of that device is probably one reason why Charles Dickens was interested in his plays. Jonson has that same metonymy of character that Dickens achieved by depending on the reaader's recollection of a repeated detail. For example, in *Our Mutual Friend* (chap. 4), after we have seen the beauteous Miss Bella Wilfer and her lovely shoulders a few times, Dickens can get a delicious

From *Jonson and Elizabethan Comedy: Essays in Dramatic Rhetoric.* © 1978 by the Henry E. Huntington Library and Art Gallery. Publishers Press, 1978.

effect with "in the Wilfer household, where a monotonous appearance of Dutch-cheese at ten o'clock in the evening has been rather frequently commented on by the dimpled shoulders of Miss Bella." Bobadill, Tucca, and Ananias receive this kind of reduction, too, in a single trick of speech. By the last act of *Alchemist* Jonson is sure to get a laugh, and perhaps some appreciation for his skill, from a series of mere fragments of speech, each absolutely perfect in its power to recall the speaker's whole dramatic and compulsive self.

> LOVEWIT: Gentlemen, what is the matter? Whom do you seek?
> MAMMON. The chemical cozener.
> SURLY: And the captain pandar.
> KASTRIL: The nun my suster.
> MAMMON: Madam Rabbi.
> ANANIAS: Scorpions,
>   And caterpillars.

Each is so imprisoned in his mode of speech that together the accusations sound ridiculously inconsistent. Again the repetition works in several ways, and almost formulaic speech does much of it.

An instructive test of this technique may be given to potentially painful and serious situations that Jonson renders comic, and *Volpone* lends itself to this test particularly well because many critics have doubted that it is really a comedy. Others come to its defense by suggesting that it is black comedy or comedy turning into satire or tragedy. I find both opinions misleading for they are based on too narrow a reading of certain speeches.

I. CORVINO'S COMIC ITERATIONS

The most intensely obsessed character in the play, Corvino, reacts in violent language to Celia's innocent glance out the window when she drops her handkerchief to Scoto. Meanwhile the audience sees the action in a larger frame of reference, knowing that there will be important consequences of her apparently harmless act, entangling her in Volpone's web of desire and provoking him more. In act 2, scene 4 we have seen Volpone back at his palace, fresh from his masquerade as Scoto, crying out to Mosca that he has been wounded, devastatingly wounded, by Celia's eyes. He is possessed, too, and will do something about it more effectively than Corvino. But within the immediate scene that follows (2.5), given only what Corvino and Celia know, her husband reacts strangely. Should the audience consider his speeches with complete seriousness? His hideous jealousy, his moral degradation, loss of reasonable control, and almost fiendish cruelty could make him bestial in this bestial world. But Jonson takes pains here to insure that Corvino is as ludicrous as he is savage.

Corvino's reaction is ridiculously incompatible with what he saw happen. Celia simply stepped to the window, looked out, and tossed her handkerchief with some money to buy the medicine (she innocently thought). In return she was to be given a beauty powder. In Corvino's twisted imagination Scoto and his crew enacted a sexual intrigue, like Signor Flaminio trying to seduce Franciscina in the *commedia dell' arte*. The evidence before him clearly does not support his sudden, paranoiac conclusion, nor does our opinion of his wisdom rise because we know for a fact that he is accidentally correct in this case. His response is no more the sensible one than Sir Politic Would-be's predictable interpretation of the episode. In answer to the question, "What should this mean, Sir Pol?" he says, "Some trick of state, believe it," and he will go home to protect himself from the design upon him. Pol thinks that all his letters may have been intercepted— his automatic response, his metonymic association.

Alone with Celia, Corvino raves like a madman, magnifying the details of the encounter. Hers are "itching ears," Peregrine and Pol were "old, unmarried, noted lechers," leering satyrs. She "fanned her favors forth" to give the "hot spectators satisfaction." He imagines that she loves Scoto's copper rings, his saffron jewel "with the toadstone in't." Surely he has a fixation on his approaching cuckoldry, for he repeatedly invites his simple wife to entertain the idea of "mounting."

> well, you shall have him, yes!
> He shall come home, and minister unto you
> The fricace for the mother. Or, let me see,
> I think you'd rather mount; would you not mount?
> Why, if you'll mount, you may; yes truly, you may.

He continues another twenty lines, speculating on how she will receive her lover, how Corvino will get revenge, killing her father, mother, brother, and all her family, and he imagines in remarkable detail and heavy accentual, alliterative verse how he will kill Celia. All because of a few glances.

> I should strike
> This steel into thee, with as many stabs
> As thou wert gazed upon with goatish eyes.

Celia repeatedly points out the absurdity of his judgment, but he lunges to more preposterous extremes.

Up to this moment, an actor could treat Corvino's jealousy seriously, uncomplicated by any other mood, but the next long speech must cause jealousy to topple into mad foolishness when he specifies the new restraints he will put on her. By comparison with his new decrees his earlier restraints seem liberal, and the repetition is obviously funny to us but not to him.

> First, I will have this bawdy light dammed up:
> And till't be done, some two or three yards off.
> I'll chalk a line, o'er which, if thou but chance
> To set thy desp'rate foot, more hell, more horror.
> More wild remorseless rage shall seize on thee.
> Than on a conjurer, that had heedless left
> His circle's safety ere his devil was laid.

He will lock a chastity belt on her, and he will keep her standing backwards.

> Thy lodging shall be backwards, thy walks backwards,
> Thy prospect—all be backwards, and no pleasure
> That thou shalt know, but backwards.
>
> (2.5.1–61)

She cannot even "snuff the air" of the "rank and sweaty" passerby, and if she so much as looks at the window, he will tear her apart—make an anatomy of her, dissect her body himself, and read a lecture on it "to the city and in public."

The effect of his exaggerated threats and prescriptions must be ridiculous, and Jonson has clearly signaled this to the actor and audience with absurd details like the "bawdy light" and her "desp'rate foot" over the asinine chalk line. As her offense was in showing her face, he insists on the nonsense of her lodging backwards, walking backwards, looking backwards, and enjoying her pleasures backwards. There may be a perverse suggestion in the last, that Corvino might enjoy his goatish pleasures backwards with her. At any rate, the grotesque image that caps the speech—his revenge for a glance—combines the comic and grotesque sadism of the man in an indissoluble union. He is impelled toward a public anatomy of his shame in an effort to save his honor and reputation!

Corvino habitually tries to persuade by threats so grotesque that they rebound upon him, exposing his ridiculous compulsions. Flaying and anatomizing her in public is not his only threat and exhibition; the most extreme comes later when he tries to push her into bed with Volpone.

> Be damned!
> Heart, I will drag thee hence home by the hair,
> Cry thee a strumpet through the streets; rip up
> Thy mouth, unto thine ears, and slit thy nose
> Like a raw rotchet. . . . Death! I will buy some slave,
> Whom I will kill, and bind thee to him alive,
> And at my window hang you forth, devising
> Some monstrous crime, which I, in capital letters,
> Will eat into thy flesh with aquafortis
> And burning corrosives, on this stubborn breast.
> $\qquad$ (3.7.95–105)

It is as if Corvino has designed an emblem or impress for himself here (as Volpone designed one for himself, "a fox / Stretched on the earth with fine delusive sleights, / Mocking a gaping crow," 1.2.94–96). In fact Corvino is the slave about to commit a monstrous crime, dramatically printed in capital letters with burning corrosive for us all to see. His favorite phrase is, suitably, "Be damned!"

The dramatic force of his speeches lies not just in the moment. They have built toward such an outrageous passion in order to make Mosca's interview with him (2.6) more impressive. Mosca moves this man by doubly persuasive rhetoric to offer his beautiful young wife to Volpone, proving that Corvino's greed must be truly out of this world. Within the next hundred lines Mosca must turn Corvino's mind completely over and leave him prepared to urge his wife to do what he most feared she would do. The powerful words and feelings that cause this flip-flop surely reduce Corvino to a caricature, an instrument of Mosca's sport. The focal points of laughter in scene 6 are precisely those details that recall Corvino's obsessive speeches a few minutes earlier, and they are punctuated by his exclamations and the "uncanny" repetitions. Scoto's oil is said to have brought Volpone to consciousness ("Death! that damned mountebank!"), his fricace helped the process ("Pox o' that fricace"), a group of physicians plan to use a young woman for a medical experiment ("Death to my hopes!"). A few minutes ago he declared that his wife's meddling with a quack was "Death of my honor," but now it is a "point of honor" to show that he is not jealous, and of course, he hopes to outwit the "covetous wretch," Doctor Lupo, who offered his virgin daughter for the experiment.

Repetition of other details heightens our perception of Corvino's compulsion to act even though he contradicts himself. He had wanted to hang a chastity belt on Celia to make a circle of safety like the conjurer who tries to deal with the devil; now he will use his wife's body to conjure heat in Volpone, albeit Mosca assures him that the patient is so sick and so impotent that no "incantation can raise his spirit" in that long unused part. Whereas before, Corvino would stab everyone of Celia's relatives, now he will use her to "cut all the throats" of Volpone's clients. In a deeper sense, he is the compulsive husband as much now as before, when he directs Celia to put on her best clothers and choicest jewels:

> We are invited to a solemn feast
> At old Volpone's, where it shall appear
> How far I am free from jealousy or fear.
>   (2.7.16–18)

His neurotic fear makes him vulnerable to precisely Mosca's kind of appeal, so he plays the clown, pretending to show his liberty when we know his bondage.

II. Exuberant Speech

Comic dialogue has other values aside from dramatic pressure and repetition, that are more independent of their representational use. They are intrinsic values especially important to comedy because individual speeches need to keep up a liveliness, a high-spirited sense of pleasure that is not expected in serious drama. Lyly, Congreve, and Oscar Wilde sustained that delicate excitement by a fusillade of wit. "It's a question that would puzzle an arithmetician . . . whether the Bible saves more souls in Westminster Abbey, or damns more in Westminster Hall," says Valentine in *Love for Love*, and no one is expected to answer; simply a clever observation, reflecting upon the interchangeable uses of religion, that leads to nothing else. In this sense the quip represents, vaguely, Valentine's pretended madness, a kind of extreme religious melancholy, used as a stalking horse from behind which he launches his witticisms, though the immediate pleasure of a clever antithesis like this outweighs its small dramatic function.

Some comic playwrights like George Bernard Shaw and Jonson, though they were witty men themselves, used formal repartee or facetious jests sparingly in their plays. Dryden considered this a defect of Jonson's art, for repartee, the very soul of conversation, is the "greatest grace of comedy." There may be "much acuteness in a thing well said; but there is more in a quick reply." Dryden notwithstanding, it is possible to maintain a gayety in dialogue, at the same time avoiding the studied artificiality of wit, by exaggeration, mock pretentiousness, flattery, self-praise, brilliant over-simplifications, and all the tricks of the monologist. Verbal excitement in Shaw and Jonson does just that, without neat, balanced phrases or fine little ironies and arch whimsies that we associate with silvery laughter. Instead, they rely upon a flood of words, an energy of expression that seems to come from strong convictions. Since they do not write genteel comedy, the lack of wit should be no surprise; their more vital comedy needs greater force of expression.

In some characters like Zeal of the Land Busy, Ananias, Wasp, and Captain Tucca or like Shaw's Sergius, Ferrovius, Alfred Doolittle, and Mrs. Hushabye the flow of words is so impelled with energy that it suggests demonic possession. But more intelligent characters like Face, Mosca, and Truewit or Jack Tanner, Andrew Undershaft, and Captain Bluntschli use vigorous language as an instrument of power and assurance. Their dialogue has its appropriateness therefore, since it helps to depict the characters of confidence men, mockers, rogues, and supermen, who are above or outside conventional morality. But its intrinsic vitality is its immediate force, its surplus value, which bribes the audience to accept their meaning for more than it may be really worth.

When Jonson spoke in his own voice, he habitually avoided high–flown style, preferring the astringent tone and precision of the plain style. He was different from Shaw, for in this mode Jonson usually steered away from superlatives or sweeping generalizations. But when he praised a great beauty or a great virtue, he could be more expansive, and when he depicted zany comic figures he gave freer play to his powers. It has long been recognized, for example, that Jonson was particularly disposed toward hyperbole in his middle comedies, with his ability to out-Marlowe Marlowe. After all, he coined the phrase "Marlowe's mighty line," and later in the century it was reported of "Mr. Marlowe . . . whose mighty lines Mr. Benjamin Johnson (a man sensible enough of his own abilities) was often heard to say, that they were examples fitter for admiration than for parallel." Jonson did not try to equal Marlowe, but to turn his extravagance to comic use in such memorable passages as Sir Epicure Mammon's description of his sexual fantasies, making a parody of the heroic imagination. Indeed, hyperbole is generally pervasive in Jonson's plays and not confined to isolated examples. It is especially interesting to see how, in terms of poetic theory, his comic style was related to the language of praise.

Jonson practiced formal praise seriously in his masques and poems, and there he distinguished praise from flattery, especially in the poems. Honest commendation called for the utmost scrupulousness on the part of the poet: 1) the contemplation of an ideal type, the idea of his subject that a man should live up to; 2) the establishment of the poet's true relation to the object of praise, his sincere feelings, and his lack of ulterior motives; 3) expression in restrained but dignified language, appropriate to the thing praised and accompanied by little unspoken compliments and apt analogies; 4) appeal to the literal truth, the actual subject, or the man himself. In the masques Jonson especially liked to insist on this last point, that the true perfection of someone's virtues was finally inexpressible; we must go beyond art to the real thing. In the presence of the king and queen all rhetoric seemed pale, all other loves to be imitations, as in *Love's Welcome at Bolsover.*

Conversely, flattery was for Jonson the worst poetic sin, and when a poet praised someone who was later revealed to be unworthy, he felt that he had betrayed his art. That is probably what disturbed him about the Essex-Somerset-Overbury affair, as much as his personal connection with Sir Thomas Overbury. His masque, *Hymenaei,* had praised the young earl and his wife for their "auspicious" marriage in 1606, but in 1612–13 the couple was involved in a scandal including divorce, adultery, and finally murder. His only consolation was that such praise survives as a libel on the subject more than on the poet. In the words of the epigram "To My Muse," the poet commits "fierce idolatry" to a great image when he praises a worthless lord. In contrition he expects his new muse will instruct him to write things "manly and not smelling parasite." Yet, a higher understanding of his art allows him to affirm the double-edged principle of laudatory poetry: "Who e'er is raised, / For worth he has not, he is tax'd not praised" (Epigram 65). Flattery belongs to the parasite, praise and blame to the true poet.

The language of praise in *Volpone* has important connections with this poetic strategy, for the play shows how double-edged flattery and self-approbation can become the tissue of comic dialogue. The play smells of the parasite and things unmanly, as most audiences agree, but the playful use of flattery goes beyond Jonson's practice in the epigrams or masques.

In the early scenes, inflated dialogue generates rising expectations, and these thrust the action forward, as Volpone and Mosca reach for ever more daring achievements. They first seek only presents from the clients; then they lust for the most prized possession from two clients—Corbaccio's whole estate (getting him to disinherit his son) and Corvino's beautiful wife. After an unforeseen setback, they recover all by use of Voltore's talent for legal oratory. More daring than ever, they outdo themselves by the mock death of Volpone and by their delight in vexation of the disappointed heirs. In this expanding scheme, the play's last act cannot be considered as tacked on so much as a culmination, a final outrageous yearning toward the ultimate practical joke. What started as a game of flattery and false hopes ends in a self-contained fantasy of vexation, the flatterers subverted by their own ruse and imprisoned by the self-serving and corrupt instruments of justice.

Skillful use of flattery moves this action forward, especially in the early scenes where the atmosphere is almost gay. We are first treated to an exhibition of hyperbolic congratulation in the exchanges between Mosca and Volpone. They are so terribly pleased with themselves and their clever fun that they fairly burst with exuberance in language abounding with words that suggest pleasure beyond ordinary experience. Volpone's favorite superlatives—*all, every, all things, any*—are set against the sweeping negatives—*no* and *nothing*. (Puttenham's *Art of English Poesy* describes such hyperbole as the "over-reacher" or "loud liar," and recommends it for praise, although still a figure of dissimulation that may have a false bottom.) Volpone praises his possessions as "far transcending / *All* style of joy in children, parents, friends, / Or *any* other waking dream on earth." Money is a dumb god who "gives *all* men tongues," it can do nothing, "yet mak'st men do *all things*." It levels all distinctions, is an amalgam of all good—"virtue, fame, / Honor, and *all things* else," and whoever gets money has unlimited *virtus*, "He shall be noble, valiant, honest, wise . . . what he will." It is possible to read these speeches as profane prayer because of the sprinkling of religious images, but that interpretation emphasizes a moral tone that is not yet as prominent as the exuberant boasting. (Anyway, the rhetoric of praise always tended to use religious imagery.) What matters is the emphasis here on "delights" in free invention of one's conceit.

Volpone goes on to commend his sport in getting money, and his great negative catalogues help to build an impression of extraordinary vanity. He gains in

> No common way: I use *no* trade, *no* venture;
> I wound *no* earth with plough shares, fat *no* beasts
> To feed the shambles; have *no* mills for iron,
> Oil, corn, or men, to grind 'em into powder.

After a dozen more lines in the same vein by Mosca, Volpone agrees that he "strikes truth in all," and so they proceed to set their actions above the common way, leading them to a high gratification of "all delights" (1.1.15–73).

In nearly every scene of the play, these two rogues puff each other with repeated interjections like "my beloved Mosca," "right Mosca," "thanks, kind Mosca," "good rascal," "loving Mosca," "excellent Mosca," "my divine Mosca," "exquisite Mosca," "Oh my fine devil," and "excellent varlet." "Thou art mine honor, Mosca, and my pride. My joy, my tickling, my delight!" (3.7.68–69). Mosca returns the compliments with similar but more modest praise of "your sweet nature," "sharp sir," along with his corresponding self-denigrations. He tells his master that he hopes to see Volpone lord of thousands more rich presents, and when "I am lost in blended dust, and hundred such as I am, in succession . . . You shall live still to delude these harpies." "My patron" he says in mock gratitude.

Their extravagant expressions of joy make indiscriminate use of verbal formulas for praise, such a thicket of comparatives and superlatives as *more than, better than, best, even brighter than, most,* and *too.*

> More glad than is
> The teeming earth to see the longed for sun
> Peep through the horns of the celestial Ram,
> Am I to view thy splendor, darkening his.
> (1.1.3–6)

"Even hell, with thee to boot, / Is made worth heaven." "Riches are in fortune a greater good than wisdom is in nature." But in order to outdo his praise of riches, Volpone goes one better:

> Yet, I glory
> More in the cunning purchase of my wealth
> Than in the glad possession.
> (1.1.30–32)

Subsequent speeches continue these intensifiers, as the confidence men jump from one success to an even more ambitious attempt.

> The Turk is not more sensual in his pleasures
> Than will Volpone.
>
> . . . .
>
> Why, this is better than rob churches, yet.
> (1.5.88–91)

All these exaggerations, like their preposterous games with the clients, tend to elevate the speakers' spirits, for "Good wits are greatest in extremities" (5.2.6).

The verbal energies of Volpone and Mosca are powerful enough to carry them and the audience away so that we do not think very much about the moral implications. Flattering language therefore is one of the means by which Volpone "cockers up" both his genius and our pleasure in order to "live free to all delights" that fortune calls one to (1.1.71–72). It is typical, at the departure of each client, that Volpone should leave his restraint and confinement, to let himself go.

> Oh I shall burst:
> Let out my sides, let out my sides—
>
> . . . .
>
> I cannot hold; good rascal, let me kiss thee:
> I never knew thee in so rare a humor.
>
> (1.4.132–38)

These are cues to the audience as much as expressions of his gladness. "Thou hast today outgone thyself" (1.5.85), he exclaims. And at the moment before the last climax of the play, Mosca says nearly the same thing: "We cannot think to go beyond this," while Volpone exults,

> Oh more than if I had enjoyed the wench:
> The pleasure of all woman-kind's not like it.
>
> (5.2.10–11)

So pleasure in tricks is a surrogate, superior indeed to normal sex, but not without homosexual implications.

Sometimes Volpone's alternating moods are signaled by language that hints at his helplessness without his "sweet" Mosca. Alone, he is quickly bored or depressed without the stimulation that Mosca's tongue usually supplies. As he awaits his servant's return with news of Celia, he is restless at the "wretched" long time it takes (3.3.1–2), and Lady Would-be's talk depresses him even more. But as Mosca disposes of her, his "hopes" burst forth anew.

> My spirits are returned: I am alive
> And like your wanton gamester at primero
> Whose thought has whispered to him, "Not go less,"
> Methinks I lie and draw—for an encounter.
>
> (3.5.35–39)

Thus cockered up, he will not go for less than everything. When a deeper depression comes upon him after the first trial, recalling that he had a cramp while trying to lie still on the stretcher in court, he imagines that some supernatural power struck him with a "dead" palsy. His language picks up life, however, with a series of intensifying words.

> Well, I must be merry
> And shake it off. A many of these fears
> Would put me into some villainous disease,
> Should they come thick upon me: I'll prevent 'em
> Give me a bowl of lusty wine, to fright
> This humor from my heart. (*He drinks*) Hum, hum, hum.
> 'Tis almost gone already: I shall conquer.
> Any device, now, of rare, ingenious knavery
> That would possess me with a violent laughter,
> Would make me up again! (*Drinks again*) So, so, so, so.
> This heat is life; 'tis blood, by this time: Mosca!
> (5.1.7–17)

Wine, like words, sex, and ingenious knavery, brings a new vitality.

Exuberant language also works on the willing victims, as flattery raises their hopes, like pouring oil in their ears; so Mosca says, "You know this hope is such a bait, it covers any hook" (1.4.134–35). By grand lists of things and by verbal bait, he creates their ridiculous desires for greater and greater exclusive benefits. To Voltore, he says "Only you of all the rest are [the one who] commands his love" (1.3.1–2). "All my hopes depend upon your worship" (1.3.35–36). He lists the things he has done for Voltore, emphasizing *your* in each case.

> I am a man that have not done your love
> All the worst offices: here I wear your keys,
> See all your coffers and your caskets locked,
> Keep the poor inventory of your jewels,
> Your plate and monies, am your steward, sir,
> Husband your goods here.
> (1.3.39–44)

A few minutes later he assures Corbaccio of his future success, in the same flurry of pronouns.

> Your cares, your watchings, and your many prayers,
> Your more than many gifts, your this day's present,
> And last produce your will.
> (1.4.100–102)

Corbaccio is especially excited by the signs of decay in Volpone's flesh, and each item has its familiar intensifier: "his face drawn longer," "His mouth is ever gaping, and his eyelids hang," "A freezing numbness stiffens all his joints and makes the color of his flesh like lead," "a cold sweat with a continual rheum." Corbaccio responds with rising enthusiasm: "Good . . . tis good . . . good . . . excellent, excellent. Sure I shall outlast him. This makes me young again, a score of years" (1.4.41–56). He fastens on the delusion of restored youth, but Volpone describes a moment later the real Corbaccio, by contrast, a man beyond all cares, maladies, and fear attending old age—no teeth, wracked with palsy and gout. He

> flatters his age,
> With confident belying it, hopes he may
> With charms, like Aeson, have his youth restored:
> And with these thoughts so battens, as if fate
> Would be as easily cheated on, as he,
> And all turns air.
>
> (1.4.154–59)

We should take this remark in its context as pleasant ridicule of Corbaccio; it applies to Volpone himself only when the action becomes more serious.

Corvino is cockered up with similar promises, as Mosca tells him he is "most wished for," "How happy were you, if you knew it now!" (1.5.1–2), "He still calls on you, nothing but your name is in his mouth" (1.5.8–9). And in response to Mosca's assurances, Corvino is properly appreciative, again in pronouns.

> Grateful Mosca!
> Thou art my friend, my fellow, my companion,
> My partner, and thou shalt share in all my fortunes.
>
> (1.5.79–81)

Mosca's favorite linguistic device is the stupendous heap of words, an accumulation appropriate for a play about greed. In his use of this figure Jonson's cumulative style clearly emerges. It works by asymmetrical parallelism, repetition, climax, and a singular lack of subordination or connectives, aside from *and, but, or,* and *as.* Mosca has little desire to twist his way through a periodic sentence or to pause and suspend his thought long enough to make balanced phrases, in the manner of Lyly or Congreve's characters. Logical subordination and a sense of orderly deduction from premises seem foreign to this style, because the main impression must be of the restless energy and boundless high spirits that Mosca shares with his master and their victims. His description of Voltore's dreams of success illustrates the connection between exuberant style and high expectations.

Voltore's thoughts, as he waits outside the bedroom, are depicted by an accumulation, sprinkled with the ultimate intensifiers, *last, all,* and *naught.*

> That this might be the last gift he should give;
> That this would fetch you; if you died today
> And gave him all, what he should be tomorrow;
> What large return would come of all his ventures;
> How he should worshiped be and reverenced;
> Ride with his furs and foot-cloths, waited on
> By herds of fools and clients; have clear way
> Made for his mule, as lettered as himself;
> Be called the great and learned advocate:
> And then concludes there's naught impossible.
>
> (1.2.100–109)

Emphasis on his hopes comes from the frequent *would's* and *should's* and *might's*. It builds with repeated *this's* and *what's*, along with palpable verbs, the reality almost in Voltore's grasp—*worshiped, reverenced, waited on,* and *have clear way made*—and it climaxes with the grand deification that naught's impossible.

Even when Mosca talks to himself (in his only soliloquy, 3.1.1–32), he is carried away by enthusiasm and flattered by his opinion of his own cleverness, for success has made him wanton and his "prosperous parts . . . so spring and burgeon" that he imagines he can feel the whimsy in his blood. He is so limber that he feels like skipping out of his skin, as a snake does in spring. Like Corbaccio and Volpone, therefore, when he thinks of his cleverness he feels reborn. In the long speech that follows. Mosca praises himself as the ideal parasite, the divine, Neoplatonic model of the flatterer and self-server, and the anti-Virgilian artist, opposed to the archetype of the true poet that we saw in the *Poetaster.* The style of the passage displays all the features of the figure of accumulation, or the heaping figure, as Puttenham calls it, and it stands as a counterpart of Volpone's opening praise of gold and his cunning purchase of his wealth.

As in many laudatory poems, Mosca begins with his heavenly genealogy. The perfect parasite is "dropped from above, / Not bred 'mongst clods and clodpoles here on earth." Then he proceeds to a demonstration of the universal practice of his professional art, worthy to be a "science"— and this is surely the comic puff—"All the wise world is little else . . ./ But parasites or sub-parasites." Next he makes a long, negative catalog of the inferior kinds of parasites, which he is not: not men who have the "bare town art" with no house, no family, no care, and who make up scandal to "bait" the ears of their host; not men who bow and flatter, "echo my lord" and lick away the vermin on his jacket. Mosca caps his vainglorious hymn with the inflated definition of the true flatterer. Since his exuberant metaphors were usually associated with descriptions of the whimsical imagination that controlled the melancholy aberrations of men, we are expected to see his ideal parasite as imagination personified—moreover, imagination uncontrolled by judgment. It is the faculty that can rise and stoop almost at the same time (like Volpone's spirits, and Mosca's flattery that seems humble as it is self-serving), like an arrow shot through the air, nimble as a star, able to make sharp turns like a swallow in flight,

> and be here,
> And there, and here, and yonder, all at once;
> Present to any humor, all occasion;
> And change a visor swifter than a thought!
> (3.1.26–29)

He does not have to learn such deception, for he was born with the art, and he practices it "out of most excellent nature."

Mosca's self-praise is, of course, just, because he has extraordinary charm and ability to create illusion. But at the same time it is caricature, for there can be no doubt that his monologue delineates the great vice of praising, as Jonson calls it in *Discoveries* (ll.1586–1635). There Jonson describes flatterers in terms identical with Mosca's ideal parasite. The parasite with the "town art" flatters for his bread, praising all that "my oraculous Lord does or says, be it true or false." Jonson says that the flatterer invents tales that will please, "makes baits for his Lordship's ears," he shifts to any point of the compass, affirms and denies the same statement, fitting discourse to persons and occasions. (We should note how dangerously close this attribute of the flatterers comes to Jonson's favorite theory of decorum in language, that required fitting language to the audience and the subject.) Flatterers "praise my Lord's wine and the sauce he likes; observe the cook and bottle man, while they stand in my Lord's favor, speak for a pension for them, but pound them to dust upon my Lord's least distaste of change of his palate." The basic metaphor in Jonson's account suggests appetite—the flatterers and calumniators gather scraps of discourse and devour them at one table, utter them at another. They are like magpies or swallows who "picking up filth of the house . . . carry it to their nest (the Lord's ears) and oftentimes report the lies they have fained for what they have seen and heard." Jonson concludes, "I know not truly which is worse, he that maligns all or that praises all. There is as great a vice in praising and as frequent as in detracting." Parasites specialize in lies and flattery, precisely Mosca's talents. Mosca's soliloquy praises those qualities which Jonson dispraises, and both use the same device, an accumulation. Mosca's speech, however, is different from the solemn pronouncements in *Discoveries*. It is especially lively because of his high spirits, and he tells us, in effect, that he thinks he can do anything now. The impression that the play has created suggests that this assurance is not far from the truth.

The Double View in *Volpone*

C. N. Manlove

Current discussions of the "instructive" and "delightful" elements in *Volpone* (1604) tend, variously, to accept that both are united to give a single dramatic effect. The object of this article is to reargue the case that the two elements are increasingly opposed during the play.

In common with the comedy next written by Jonson—*The Alchemist* (1610)—the subject of *Volpone* is the gulling of dupes for profit by schemers; there are many incidental points of similarity in the plots and "humours" of both plays. Yet *Volpone* has a character very different from that of *The Alchemist*. Where Jonson's story of the magnifico is set in the luxurious and exotic world of Venice, *The Alchemist* takes place in London, in the house of the bourgeois Lovewit. In *Volpone* the bumbling English traveller, self-appointed man of the world and manipulator, Sir Politic Would-be, and his wife, whose assumptions of refinement only the more surely reveal her vulgarity, point up the gulf between the English temperament and that of the supersubtle Venetians, to the advantage of the latter. The world of *Volpone* is on a far grander scale than that of *The Alchemist* or *Bartholomew Fair* (1614). Volpone has enormous wealth and is surrounded by an array of dwarves, eunuchs and parasites who minister to him and execute his purposes. He demands far more of those he gulls than Subtle and Face do in *The Alchemist*. Not only does he demand large sums of money or valuable jewels and plate, but he even demands of the obsessively jealous Corvino, his own wife. The most in this respect which Subtle and Face ask in *The*

From *Studies in English Literature 1500–1900* 19, no. 2 (Spring 1979). © 1979 by William Marsh Rice University.

Alchemist is his sister of Kastril—and her name is Pliant. Moreover, the performance in court of one of Volpone's dupes, the lawyer Voltore, goes far beyond that required of any character in the later play: when, at Volpone's instigation, he for a second time retracts a false case made by him against previous defendants, he pretends to have been possessed and feigns a fit in which he vomits out "evil spirits." The nearest we come to this performance in *The Alchemist* is Dapper's enforced sojourn in the jakes. In *The Alchemist* too the payments exacted by Face and Subtle of their clients— Mammon's andirons, the dollars of the Puritans, Drugger's tobacco or portague, Dapper's twenty nobles or his "paper with a spur-ryal in't"— are trivia by comparison, typified by the final inventory of the "confederacy":

> FACE: Mammon's ten proud; eight score before.
> The Brethern's money, this. Drugger's and Dapper's.
> What paper's that?
> DOL: The jewel of the waiting maid's,
> That stole it from her lady, to know certain—
> FACE: If she should have precedence of her mistress?
> SUBTLE: Yes.
> DOL: What box is that?
> SUBTLE: The fishwives' rings I think,
> And th'alewives' single money. Is't not, Dol?
> DOL: Yes, and the whistle that the sailor's wife
> Brought you to know and her husband were with
>   Ward.
> FACE: We'll wet it tomorrow; and our silver beakers,
> And tavern cups. Where be the French petticoats,
> And girdles, and hangers?
> SUBTLE: Here, i' the trunk,
> And the bolts of lawn.
> FACE: Is Drugger's damask there?
> And the tobacco?
>
>   (5.4.108–21)

With these vulgar commodities we can be more familiar, as indeed with the wishes of most of the gulls. But with the desire of the rich to be richer still, as we find it in *Volpone,* there is much less scope for this level of engagement.

The motives of the gullers are also different. Volpone loves wealth not because it gives material or social advancement, but because it gives power:

he is in his way a megalomaniac. He is by no means a miser, for he keeps an extensive house and has luxurious tastes. He simply worships money because of its magnetic strength of attraction, its power to break all other links which stand in its way and draw in its victims. Wealth is seen as the focus of the universe:

> Hail the world's soul, and mine! More glad than is
> The teeming earth to see the longed-for sun
> Peep through the horns of the celestial Ram,
> Am I, to view thy splendor darkening his;
> That lying here, amongst my other hoards,
> Showst like a flame by night, or like the day
> Struck out of chaos, when all darkness fled
> Unto the center. O thou son of Sol,
> But brighter than thy father, let me kiss,
> With adoration, thee, and every relic
> Of sacred treasure in this blessed room.
>
> (1.1.3–13)

Every other value is transcended, swallowed by wealth, until riches become God himself. Volpone sees the substance that is gold, like God, reducing all else to shadow by its sheer facticity:

> Thou being the best of things, and far transcending
> All style of joy in children, parents, friends,
> Or any other waking dream on earth.
>
> (1.1.16–18)

What fascinates him is the image of the stasis of wealth that puts all other things in a state of flux, the sheer inertia of this mineral which engrosses to itself all states of existence or value that are above it in the scale of being:

> Dear saint
> Riches, the dumb god that givst all men tongues,
> That canst do nought, and yet mak'st men do all things;
> The price of souls; even hell, with thee to boot,
> Is made worth heaven! Thou are virtue, fame,
> Honor, and all things else. Who can get thee,
> He shall be noble, valiant, honest, wise.
>
> (1.1.21–27)

In these lines Olympian detachment combines with complete commitment: Volpone speaks in apparently detached wonder at the power of gold and yet can testify to that power over himself. In the last three lines he is saying both, "You subsume all value," and "Look how benighted man is, that he will attribute to one who is wealthy all spiritual value." This double position of involvement and ironic distance is the key to Volpone's motivation in the play: it enables him to jest while he is in earnest, to laugh at the follies of the gulls who seek his money while he delights in the power of, and homage paid to, his wealth. The essence is to do nothing while others do everything: as his gold is "lying here," so too does Volpone for most of the play on his sickbed, attended by a constant succession of would-be heirs. The stress is on the enclosed nature of his world: he does not go out to get his wealth, for it comes to him without his stir; he does not have an impact upon the outside world, for that world is pleased to visit him:

> I gain
> No common way: I use no trade, no venture;
> I wound no earth with ploughshares; fat no beasts
> To feed the shambles; have no mills for iron,
> Oil, corn, or men, to grind 'em into powder;
> I blow no subtle glass; expose no ships
> To threat'nings of the furrow-facèd sea;
> I turn no monies in the public bank,
> Nor usure private.
> (1.1.32–40)

What begins as a picture of the sophisticated manner in which he makes his gold turns into a protestation of innocence—"I do not interfere with the world." But it is interesting that he conceives the hurting which he has avoided more as a hurting of things, not of people: the earth is not wounded except under the terms of the pathetic fallacy, or unless one considers the earth to be animate. Fatting beasts to feed the shambles is not generally considered cruelty. The upset of hierarchy behind Volpone's words is seen in the way he speaks of "iron/Oil, corn, or men" as the same sort of commodity for mills and in his picture of the mills as causing suffering to inanimate substance the same way they cause suffering to men ("grind 'em into powder"). Thus when he speaks of ships rather than of men exposed "To threat'nings of the furrow facèd sea," we are inclined to take the ships simply as vessels rather than as vessels containing men—an inclination reinforced by the animate status given to the sea. Aware, no doubt, that this protestation of innocence is somewhat misdirected, Mosca now turns it to more human contexts:

> No, sir, nor devour
> Soft prodigals. You shall ha' some will swallow
> A melting heir as glibly as your Dutch
> Will pills of butter, and ne'er purge for't;
> Tear forth the fathers of poor families
> Out of their beds, and coffin them, alive,
> In some kind, clasping prison, where their bones
> May be forthcoming, when the flesh is rotten.
> But, your sweet nature doth abhor these courses;
> You loathe the widow's or the orphan's tears
> Should wash your pavements, or their piteous cries
> Ring in your roofs, and beat the air for vengeance.
>
> (1.1.40–51)

He covers a range of impact from the soft prodigals, who might deserve their loss, to the innocent, who would not: again the portrayal of Volpone's guiltlessness is founded on his self-enclosure, not on any distinction he makes between those who deserve fleecing and those who do not. Moreover, in the very manner which Mosca paints the refusal of his master's "sweet nature" to seize on the undeserving and cause pain to their families, along with his equal refusal to "devour" prodigals and "melting heir[s]," we see that no such sweet motive really exists; we are nearer the truth in Volpone's objection to any invasion of his privacy by tears washing his pavements or by piteous cries ringing in his roofs (an objection portrayed in his reactions to Lady Would-be throughout the play).

What we have in Volpone is a man whose scale of values is entirely perverted by money, but who, at the same time, without applying the condition to himself, is able to see how wealth overthrows all values in other people. He is a man who has taken on an Olympian position, but who himself is one of those he mocks—a man who is in a fundamentally ironic position throughout the play. Hence, a part of his weakness is that he who manipulates others can himself be manipulated. Mosca is not plotting Volpone's ruin when he raises his interest in Corvino's wife Celia in terms of her likeness to gold; he is playing on his master's Pavlovian responses:

> Bright as your gold! and lovely as your gold!
> VOLPONE: Why had not I known this before?
> MOSCA: Alas, sir,
> Myself but yesterday discovered it.
> VOLPONE: How might I see her?

MOSCA: O, not possible;
> She's kept as warily as is your gold,
> Never does come abroad, never takes air
> But at a window.
>
>   (1.5.114–20)

Celia, spiritually Volpone's opposite, is like him and his wealth in that she never goes out to the world (though in her case she is imprisoned). Yet, this portrait of her by Mosca draws Volpone to abandon his usual posture: he is forced to go out to someone rather than have them come to him. That inconsistency is in fact the beginning of his undoing.

    Like his master, Mosca is at pains to disconnect himself from the world, even from himself:

> Success hath made me wanton. I could skip
> Out of my skin, now, like a subtle snake,
> I am so limber. O! your parasite
> Is a most precious thing, dropped from above,
> Not bred 'mongst clods and clodpolls, here on earth.
>
>   (3.1.5–9)

He goes on to distinguish himself from inferior sorts of parasites whom he sees as tied to the earth and to pleasing the senses of their masters:

> I mean not those that have your bare town-art,
> To know who's fit to feed'em; have no house,
> No family, no care, and therefore mold
> Tales for men's ears, to bait that sense; or get
> Kitchen-invention, and some stale receipts
> To please the belly, and the groin; nor those,
> With their court-dog-tricks, that can fawn and fleer,
> Make their revènue out of legs and faces,
> Echo my lord, and lick away a moth.
>
>   (3.1.14–22)

In some degree, by thus refusing the conventional image of the parasite, Mosca is denying that he is, finally, dependent on his master in the way that others are—a prognostic of his later truancy. The picture of his own class of parasite which follows continues the idea of separation from the earth in the vision of his movements in terms of an aerial being:

> But your fine, elegant rascal, that can rise
> And stoop, almost together, like an arrow;
> Shoot through the air as nimbly as a star;
> Turn short as doth a swallow; and be here,
> And there, and here, and yonder, all at once;
> Present to any humour, all occasion;
> And change a visor swifter than a thought.
>
> (3.1.22–29)

In the last two lines the notion of constant metamorphosis is so pitched as to suggest total loss of any inner and fixed identity. Indeed it is by constant movement, rather than the stasis of other parasites, that Mosca characterizes himself—an interesting contrast with Volpone's praise of his gold or with his own supine position for most of the play. Mosca further separates true parasites from the idea of earthliness or from any public dependency when he makes a Horatian distinction between those parasites who are born dependent and those who have to learn the craft:

> This is the creature had the art born with him;
> Toils not to learn it, but doth practice it
> Out of most excellent nature: and such sparks
> Are the true parasites, others but their zanies.
>
> (3.1.30–33)

The true parasite is not dependent on anything outside himself for the knowledge of his craft; we are reminded of Volpone's severance from the world.

Both Volpone and Mosca have a form of creative delight in their schemes: the gulling of Corvino, Corbaccio and Voltore is engineered not so much for gain as for the pleasure that results from skillfully-managed deception and for the mirth that arises, whether from the success of the deceptions themselves or from the way that the gulls are only too ready to assist in their own duping. After Mosca has persuaded Corbaccio to disinherit his son and make Volpone his heir, expecting that out of gratitude for such generosity the dying Volpone will in turn make Corbaccio his heir, Volpone is almost beside himself with laughter:

> O, I shall burst!
> Let out my sides, let out my sides.
> MOSCA: Contain

> Your flux of laughter, sir. You know this hope
> Is such a bait it covers any hook.
> VOLPONE: O, but thy working, and thy placing it!
> I cannot hold; good rascal, let me kiss thee.
> I never knew thee in so rare a humor.
>
> (1.4.132–38)

Typical of their relationship is the mobility with which Mosca engineers the fun for the static Volpone to enjoy, and typically, too, he cunningly disclaims responsibility and dupes his master:

> Alas, sir, I but do as I am taught;
> Follow your grave instructions; give 'em words;
> Pour oil into their ears, and send them hence.
> VOLPONE: 'Tis true, 'tis true.
>
> (1.4.139–42)

This delight in creativity, however perverse, gives enormous zest and energy to the play. Such energy is missing from *The Alchemist,* where the gulling of people who believe in the powers of alchemy is carried on specifically as a business venture for gain by the league of Dol, Face and Subtle.

It is an energy which, however immoral by all the canons, themes or imagery of the play, threatens to upset the norms invoked. Here it is worth contrasting Volpone with the luxur of *The Alchemist,* Sir Epicure Mammon. When Volpone is attempting to seduce the virtuous Celia, he tries to sway her with a picture of the sensuous delights they may both share:

> See, behold,
> [*Pointing to his treasure.*]
> What thou art queen of; not in expectation,
> As I feed other, but possessed and crowned.
> See, here, a rope of pearl, and each more orient
> Than that the brave Egyptian queen caroused;
> Dissolve and drink 'em. See, a carbuncle
> May put out both the eyes of our St. Mark;
> A diamond would have bought Lollia Paulina
> When she came in like star-light, hid with jewels
> That were the spoils of provinces; take these,
> And wear, and lose 'em: yet remains an earring
> To purchase them again, and this whole state.
> A gem but worth a private patrimony
> Is nothing; we will eat such at a meal.

The heads of parrots, tongues of nightingales,
The brains of peacocks, and of estriches
Shall be our food, and, could we get the phoenix,
Though nature lost her kind, she were our dish.

                                        (3.7.188–205)

Unnatural, of course, but beautiful—and alive. The rhythm almost enacts
Mosca's picture of the true parasite, rising, stopping, shooting and turning.
The run-on lines make these pleasures mobile, not stagnant, as do the rising
and dipping rhythms: "See, behold. . . . / Dissolve and drink 'em"; "See,
a carbuncle / . . . That were the spoils of provinces" (not quite a full close,
followed by the dolphin-like rhythm of "take these, / And wear, and lose
'em: yet remains an earring / To purchase them again, and this whole state").
Compare this with Mammon:

I will have all my beds blown up, not stuffed:
Down is too hard. And then mine oval room
Filled with such pictures as Tiberius took
From Elephantis, and dull Aretine
But coldly imitated. Then, my glasses
Cut in more subtle angles, to disperse
And mutiply the figures as I walk
Naked between my succubae. My mists
I'll have of perfume, vapored 'bout the room,
To loose our selves in; and my baths like pits
To fall into; from whence we will come forth
And roll us dry in gossamer and roses.

                                        (2.2.41–52)

The rhythm is no longer various, but stops and starts in short breaths,
flopping inert at each cadence: "Down is too hard," "From Elephantis,"
"But coldly imitated," "To loose our selves in," "To fall into." Where in
Volpone's lines the partial cadences come on significant injunctions, here
we see them fall on mere desultory afterthoughts, "Down is too hard,"
"From Elephantis," "and dull Aretine / But coldly imitated." Each item is
one in a list, and has a corresponding deadness: "my beds," "And then
mine oval room," "Then, my glasses," "my succubae," "My mists," "my
baths"; and his continual use of "my" limits his pleasure by possession,
where Volpone's impersonal pleasures seem more independent and alive.
It seems apt that the element of collapse—losing, falling and rolling—should
become explicit in the last lines. Mammon's speech continually deflates

itself rhythmically, pointing up not only his limited sensual capacity, but puncturing the absurdity of his pictures—"I will have all my beds blown up, not stuffed; / Down is too hard," "multiply the figures as I walk / Naked between my succubae" (suggesting sudden detumescence).

Other features in *Volpone* besides the energy and creative delight of both Volpone and Mosca make our—and Jonson's—attitude to them more complex than simple condemnation, although the imagery and their thematic placing by such standards as inversion of value or self-enclosure ask us to condemn them. For one thing, all the would-be heirs whom Volpone and Mosca gull are portrayed either as disgusting and depraved birds of prey (Corbaccio, Corvino and Voltore) or as vulgar fools (Lady Would-be), so that we can be led to feel that their manipulation given Volpone and Mosca a certain moral credit, however much they share their standards of value. Secondly, the energy and wit of Volpone and Mosca, when compared to the stupid monomanias of their victims, make us admire the former for reasons which have little to do with morality, in precisely the way that we admire a fine performance.

What then of Jonson's view? In *The Alchemist* the schemer Face is forgiven at the end for his practices when the master of the house returns, and that master's name is Lovewit. Of course, neither the deeds nor the mind of Face are in any way as corrupt as those of Volpone, and there is less to forgive; however, the name, Lovewit, nonetheless reveals the draw on Jonson himself to admire a scheme well and wittily handled. We may also observe that his bringing in the virtuous innocents in *Volpone* may well have been the product of a sense that the play was getting up and walking away with the moral nail; conversely, from his dedicatory Epistle, we know how uneasy Jonson subsequently was at the way he hammered it down again. As we have said, the effect of surrounding Volpone and Mosca with evil and stupid characters is to make them the more admirable, however much their language and attitudes may reveal moral perversion: it may be that, aware of this, Jonson tried to make sure of damning Volpone and Mosca by having them hurt innocence as well. The result, as has often been remarked, is unfortunate: Celia and Bonario, not belonging to the world of the action, come as a jolt, not least in their language:

> Forbear, foul ravisher! libidinous swine!
> *He leaps out from where* MOSCA *had placed him.*
> Free the forced lady, or thou diest, impostor.
> But that I am loth to snatch thy punishment
> Out of the hand of justice, thou shouldst yet

> Be made the timely sacrifice of vengeance,
> Before this altar, and this dross, thy idol.
> Lady, let's quit the place, it is the den
> Of villainy; fear nought, you have a guard;
> And he ere long shall meet his just reward.
>
> (3.7.267–75)

This language recalls the stridency of the brothers of the Lady in Milton's *Comus;* it has even the smack of some of Jonson's Puritanical figures about it. That Jonson feels the need to insert such a direct judgment into the play suggests that he feels Volpone to be flying above moral censure.

What control Jonson has over Volpone and Mosca comes as we have seen through the imagery of perversion; it should also come through the plot. For at the end Jonson tells us through the First Advocate that the play has demonstrated a process whereby evil eventually always destroys itself: "Mischiefs feed / Like beasts, till they be fat, and then they bleed" (5.12.150–51). The point is that Volpone and Mosca are not to be stopped by outside forces (Bonario and Celia are easily outwitted and imprisoned thanks to the twisted testimony of Volpone's dupes in court), but stopped by a process which will more fully educate the reader in the nature of evil, a process involving spontaneous combustion. First Volpone, having heard of the beauties of Corvino's wife Celia, goes forth disguised to see her. Then Mosca eventually succeeds in persuading Corvino to bring her to his master at a fixed time. Meanwhile Mosca brings Corbaccio's son Bonario to overhear his father disinherit him before Volpone (and so perhaps be fired to slay his parent, leaving Volpone heir), but when he arrives at Volpone's house he finds that Corvino, anxious to make certain of his chances, has come with Celia before he was due. Mosca therefore places the now suspicious Bonario out of hearing in a book gallery, hoping to keep him there and to delay Corbaccio's approach while Volpone interviews Celia. Nevertheless, Bonario does overhear Volpone with Celia, and the first court cast must then ensue if he is to be silenced.

We may at this stage ask whether Mosca might not have sent Corvino home again rather than compound his difficulties with a "Well, now there's no helping it, stay here"; and we may too ask why Mosca is wrong in his calculation that Bonario will not hear anything from the gallery (we are not told that he has come any nearer, but that *"he leaps out from where Mosca had placed him,"* 3.7.268).

In court Bonario and Celia are both discredited, not only through the machinations of Volpone's dupes, particularly the lawyer Voltore, but thorough the corrupt timeserving nature of the advocates; outside factors will not be able to destroy Volpone. When Volpone returns from court, he says,

> Well, I am here, and all this brunt is past.
> I ne'er was in dislike with my disguise
> Till this fled moment. Here, 'twas good, in private,
> But in your public—*Cavè,* whilst I breathe.
>
> (5.1.1–4)

But instead of resolving to lie quiet for a time and consolidate his success, he decides to proceed even further in his schemes. His reason is that if he did not he might fall ill of his fears:

> A many of these fears
> Would put me into some villainous disease
> Should they come thick upon me. I'll prevent 'em.
> Give me a bowl of lusty wine to fright
> This humor from my heart. Hum, hum, hum! *He drinks.*
> 'Tis almost gone already; I shall conquer.
>
> (5.1.8–13)

Yet he does not stop there:

> Any device, now, of rare, ingenious knavery
> That would possess me with a violent laughter,
> Would make me up again.
>
> (5.1.14–16)

This scheme, of course, eventually becomes one of making Mosca his heir. The motivation is clearly tenuous. That the cautious fox should so risk himself with another plot goes against the grain of what we expect; that he should attempt this scheme even when most of the unanticipated motive for so doing has been removed by the drink is even more hard to accept. Mosca, when now called for, puts the first point:

> We must here be fixed;
> Here we must rest. This is our masterpiece;
> We cannot think to go beyond this
>
> (5.2.12–14)

and Volpone later is astonished at how we could bave been so foolish:

> To make a snare for mine own neck! And run
> My head into it wilfully, with laughter!
> When I had newly 'scaped, was free and clear!
> Out of mere wantonness! O, the dull devil
> Was in this brain of mine when I devised it.
>
> (5.11.1–5)

Even then he does not know that his scheme has allowed Mosca to betray him. One wonders how Volpone proposed to undo the trick. One solution might have been for him to have servants take him to court on a stretcher and there to claim that Mosca had locked him up and forged a will in his favour (we are told that only the name has to be filled in, 5.2.71–73). Clearly Volpone had no such notion in mind: he seems to have been determined to blow up the gulls' hopes for good, without considering what they could do against him in reply ("I will begin e'en now to vex 'em all, / This very instant," 5.2.56–57).

Again, Volpone could have used the way out just suggested when he discovers Mosca has betrayed him (and after he has just beaten his breast over his previous stupidity). Instead he goes to the court to bargain with Mosca and then, that failing, to bring down his parasite with himself by disclosing his own identity. If we are to take this behavior as typical of him, we must begin to find the name "Volpone" (the fox) a little inapposite. The more reasonable view here, however, is surely that the motivation is thin and that this thinness is unconsciously deliberate on Jonson's part. He is unwilling to show Volpone as self-destructive by any other than partly trumped-up motives.

Objections to the fifth act of the play as forced rather than natural were first expressed by Dryden in 1668 and expanded by the dramatist Richard Cumberland in 1788; Jonson himself also reveals doubts in his dedicatory Epistle. Yet modern criticism has so far attacked these views to the point where Jonas A. Barish can claim:

> The inquest opened by Dryden into the structural peculiarities
> of Act V would seem to be closed; few today would dispute
> Swinburne's and Herford's verdict, that Volpone's compulsive
> resumption of his hoaxing, far from being a desperate shift to
> galvanize a flagging plot, forms one of the master strokes of the
> action.
>
> (*Ben Jonson, "Volpone": A Casebook*)

The word "compulsive" is the key to most current opinion of what drives Volpone forwards: it is said that he is incapable of rest and is driven on to his end by poisoned creative exuberance which has grown thoroughout the play. No one, however, seems to have considered that while this may partly be true, it would better be brought home to us if Volpone had not been portrayed as he is in act 5, scene 1, where he expresses his fears at the degree to which he has already overreached himself. Nor has it been remarked that he could have saved himself even after going further and that, to this extent, the "'dull devil'" which he berates in himself continues long after its supposed dismissal-in-recognition. Moreover, there is disparity in the fact that 5.2, the first scene in the play which Volpone rather than Mosca arranges, reverses the earlier dichotomy of Volpone exerting power while static and Mosca while in motion.

Jonson could not, as we have seen, let Volpone get away with it in this play because he has, at least in the first scene, and in much of the imagery, subjected him to moral analysis. However, as he wrote he came to admire his own creation to the extent that he could not find it in him to give the creation fully adequate motives answering to the governing notion of evil being self-detonating.

Volpone

Anne Barton

In his prologue to the folio *Every Man in His Humour*, Jonson proudly declared his allegiance as a comic writer to "deedes, and language, such as men doe use," to the presentation of an "Image of the times" as decorously embodied in characters of the middle or lower class, and to a concern "with humane follies, not with crimes." *Volpone*, by common consent of contemporaries and posterity Jonson's first great comedy, contrives characteristically to ignore every one of these neoclassical prescriptions. Neither the events of the play nor the dialogue through which they are conveyed could possibly be described as "realistic," even by the standard of most other contemporary urban comedies; Volpone himself is an aristocrat, a "magnifico"; and the activities of many of the characters are criminal rather than merely ridiculous, as they had been in the Elizabethan humour plays. Jonson himself felt obliged to admit, in his preface, that the harshness of the catastrophe—Mosca consigned to the galleys, Volpone to wear out the rest of his life in fetters—was a violation of "comick *law*," justified only because of its supposed didactic efficacy. It is an obvious case of special pleading. In fact, *Volpone* was generated by *Sejanus*. It is a comedy already struggling for life amid the fitful brilliances, the tonal unevenness and oddly scattered focus of its savage predecessor, and it inherits its darkness from imperial Rome.

Both *Sejanus* and *Volpone* concern themselves with the relation between a master and his parasite, one in which patron and dependant work together for a time with devastating efficiency and success, in a partnership which

---

From *Ben Jonson, Dramatist.* © 1984 by Cambridge University Press.

allows them a seemingly effortless control over other people, until it is destroyed by a mutual violation of trust. Institutionalized justice in both plays, whether the Roman Senate or the court presided over in Venice by the Avocatori, is a farce. And there are no strong, good characters in either play who can amend as well as recognize huan viciousness and crime. Like Silius, Sabinus and Arruntius, Celia and Bonario are passive victims, people whose appeals to the heaven "that never failes the innocent," or which "could not, long, let such grosse crimes be hid" (*Volpone* 4.6.17, 5.12.98), seem remarkably misplaced. Sabinus rejected the possibility of a political revolt against Tiberius on the good Elizabethan and Jacobean grounds that

> No ill should force the subject undertake
> Against the soveraigne, more then hell should make
> The gods doe wrong. A good man should, and must
> Sit rather downe with losse, then rise unjust.
>
> (*Sejanus* 4.163–66)

In *Volpone*, this reverence for authority, however corrupt, has been transferred to the sphere of family relations. Celia remains painfully loyal to the husband who first locks her up, and then tries to prostitute her to the fox. Bonario, even more strikingly, refuses even to deny in court that he meant to kill Corbaccio, the parent who now disowns him: "I will sit downe," he says, echoing Sabinus, "and rather wish my innocence should suffer, / Then I resist the authority of a father" (4.5.112–14). Jonson's usual sensitivity to the father/son relationship renders Bonario's predicament especially emotional, but it cannot cancel out the impression—reinforced elsewhere in the play—that this honourable but somewhat priggish young man over-presents his virtue.

Sejanus had looked back wistfully to the exploits of Germanicus, to the free society presided over by Augustus, and to Brutus and Cassius, the last true Romans. *Volpone* too is constantly glancing over its shoulder to a past which, although historically more diffuse, provides an equally telling series of contrasts. In the entertainment which Mosca devises for his master in act 1, the soul of Pythagoras is said to have derived its life originally from Apollo. Although its various incarnations on the way to Pythagoras represent, of necessity, a degree of falling off, its fortunes up to that point are at least respectable. Only in more recent times has it descended to animate "oxe, and asse, cammell, mule, goat, and brock" (1.2.23) or (worse still) a Puritan brother, before taking up its present, unnatural lodging in the body of an hermaphrodite kept as a salaried oddity in Volpone's household. Like this degraded soul, the noble past is perpetually being remembered in the play for what it was, even though it tends to be invoked now for debased or trivial purposes. Volpone attempts to justify his way of acquiring wealth by paralleling his life with that lived by men in an age paradoxically called "Golden" because it had no use whatever for this metal (1.1.33–40). The false Scoto of Mantua markets a powder which, he asserts, once made Venus a goddess, although at present it serves as a hair dye for the ladies of France. At the disreputable banquet in *Poetaster*, the classical gods provided the framework for an orgy. Volpone too imagines how he and Celia will "in changed shapes, act OVIDS tales" (3.7.221), coupling in the guise of Jove and Europa, Mars and Erycine. But there is now no Virgil, no Augustus or Horace to rescue the myths from their travesties. The ceaseless gabble of Lady Would-be contrives to drag Plato, Pythagoras, Petrarach, Dante and Tasso (among others) through the dust. If the phoenix did still exist, in this fallen world, Volpone could think of nothing better to do with her than have her cooked for dinner (3.7.204–5).

During the long, serpentine uncoiling of Tiberius's letter to the Senate in act 5 of *Sejanus*, Arruntius characterizes its author in an aside as "A good fox" (l. 587). So he is and, as such, elder brother to the central figure in *Volpone*—another manipulator producing dubious artistic patterns in other people's lives. The Venice of *Volpone* seems to be populated primarily by birds: the vulture, the raven, the crow, the parrot and the hawk. Reynard stands out in it by virtue of his more complex and also ambiguous ancestry in fable, folklore and the visual arts. Even in Aesop, the fox always seems more compelling and also more fully human than his victim. He may not be very nice, but given the choice, no reader would identify with the stupid crow. Mosca the Fly is also marked off by his name from the feathered bipeds who cluster about the deathbed of the Fox. Yet flies, like birds, are winged creatures, generically different from mammals, whether foxes or human beings. Apart from the anonymous rabble of merchants, officers, magistrates, women, one notary and a servant, the remaining characters are either reduced by their names to physical abnormalities (Nano the dwarf, Castrone the eunuch, Androgyno the hermaphrodite) or else designated by abstract qualities (the heavenly Celia, Bonario the good) which in this society come to seem insubstantial and even a trifle suspect. Volpone inherits centrality and a kind of wily dignity with his name, and there turns out to be no other character in the comedy possessed of sufficient humanity to challenge his preeminence. This single, undisputed focus sets *Volpone* off both from *Sejanus* and from all the rest of Jonson's earlier, surviving plays.

John Creaser has recently argued sensitively and convincingly for a psychological complexity in the chief characters of *Volpone* usually denied them. If these are types—and, after all, most dramatic characters are—each is what Eric Bentley calls "a complex type." This is true even of Celia and Bonario, those self-righteous adolescents, and to a greater extent of Volpone himself, a man who makes the fatal mistake he does in the fifth act because he is trying to repair a newly shattered sense of vitality, self-confidence and control over his circumstances. Creaser's account of these characters offers a long overdue corrective to the view that Jonson was a man only capable, even in his greatest comedies, of caricature. The fact is that the apparent simplicity of characterization in Jonson's mature comedies is deceptive. His imaginary people are far less self-aware than most of Shakespeare's. They do not fully understand, let alone find themselves able to articulate, why they act as they do. Shakespeare works through a kind of super-realism, allowing characters insight into their own motives, and an ability to externalize complex states of mind—Angelo's response to Isabella, or Shylock's to the Christians—rarely met with in life as it is. Jonson's method is different, and in many ways truer to normal experience. Important facts, that Peregrine dreads being thought naive, that Corbaccio concentrates upon becoming Volpone's heir partly because it is a way of blinding himself to his own decrepitude and approaching death, or that Volpone has already begun to tire of the way of life he celebrates with such gusto in the opening scene, must be deduced from their behaviour as a whole, not from anything they say about themselves or each other. It is a technique dependent upon inference and suggestion, rather than Shakespearean revelation.

Another reason why the characters in *Volpone* sometimes strike readers (although rarely theatre audiences) as perplexingly flat, outlines as opposed to individuals, is that Jonson has forced them to exist in a material world so dense and detailed that it constantly threatens to overwhelm them in its sheer variety and proliferation. Mosca, sketching out Voltore's opulent future after Volpone has died, tells his dupe how he will "come to swim, in golden lard, / Up to the armes, in honny, that your chin / Is borne up stiffe, with fatnesse of the floud" (1.3.70–72). The image suggests an imminent and revolting suffocation in liquid grease, something that makes Clarence's death in the malmsey butt in *Richard III* seem almost attractive by comparison. It is central to the play. Things, in *Volpone*, the urban detritus of a civilization out of control, are perpetually on the verge of rising up to drown the people who wade and push their way through them. Relentless particularity, a finicky insistence upon itemizing and making lists, is typical of the characters. Corvino asks his wife furiously whether she was enamoured of the mountebank's

> copper rings?
> His saffron jewell, with the toade-stone in't?
> Or his imbroidred sute, with the cope-stitch,
> Made of a herse-cloth? or his old tilt-feather?
> Or his starch'd beard?
>
> (2.5.11–15)

Scoto becomes the sum of his parts, an aggregate of details, each one of which has been observed with such preternatural clarity that it takes on an independent life of its own, pressing against the sense of this man as a unified entity. Corvino dissolves Scoto's elixir too into its ingredients: "a sheepes gall, a rosted bitches marrow, / Some few sod earewigs, pounded caterpillers, / A little capons grease, and fasting spittle" (2.6.18–20), while Lady Would-be assures the supposed invalid that

> Seed-pearle were good now, boild with syrrope of apples,
> Tincture of gold, and corrall, citron-pills,
> Your elicampane roote, mirobalanes
>
> . . . .
>
> Burnt silke, and amber, you have muscadell
> Good i' the house
>
> . . . .
>
> Some *english* saffron (halfe a dram would serve)
> Your sixteene cloves, a little muske, dri'd mints,
> Buglosse, and barley-meale
>
> . . . .
>
> And these appli'd, with a right scarlet-cloth.
>
> (3.4.52–63)

Volpone himself, wooing Celia, passes from itemizing a menu—"heads of parrats, tongues of nightingales, / The braines of peacoks, and of estriches" (3.7.202–3)—to listing the components of a fantastic bath oil which brings together essence of roses, violets and july-flowers with the milk of unicorns and panthers' breath, all dissolved in Cretan wines (ll. 213–16). Sir Politic Would-be, on every one of his appearances, seems to be rummaging through the contents of some gothic lumber-room of the imagination, turning out toothpicks and baboons, oranges, musk-melons, apricots, porpoises and lion-whelps, tinderboxes, onions, sprats, frayed stockings and Selsey cockles. There is a sense in which Mosca's inventory in the third scene of act 5 ("Turkie carpets, nine . . . Two sutes of bedding, tissew . . .

Of cloth of gold, two more . . . Of severall vellets, eight . . . " (5.3.6–7) is the single most representative act of the play.

An obsessive interest in things, in grotesque, unrelated detail, is often the stock in trade of the satirist, a man out to chastise the world for its incoherence. Equally obvious is the tendency for writers with a covert interest in disorder for its own sake to be drawn towards a mode which allows them to diagnose with apparent severity a public malaise they themselves have taken private delight in for years. Jonson's own predisposition towards the bizarre and peculiar emerges clearly in his conversations with Drummond. It is also recorded in his early work, both nondramatic and dramatic. But *Volpone* manages to subsume it to a single artistic purpose, and make it telling as never before. When Shakespeare indulges himself in list-making in *A Midsummer Night's Dream*—allowing old Egeus to enumerate all the love-tokens Lysander might have bestowed upon Hermia ("bracelets of thy hair, rings, gawds, conceits, / Knacks, trifles, nosegays, sweetmeats," 1.1.33–34), counting up all the obstacles that have ever threatened true love (1.1.135–42), the kinds of wild beast which might conceivably wake Titania (2.1.180–81), or burying Bottom alive under a deluge of mulberries, dewberries, apricots, honey-bags, grapes and green figs (3.1.166–68)—the effect is essentially cohesive, a paean of praise to the inexhaustible variety but also the underlying harmony of a fresh, natural world. Even Egeus's hypothetical love-charms seem unstudied and innocent by comparison with Corvino's notion that Celia's fancy might have been ensnared by an "imbroidred sute, with the cope-stitch, / Made of a herse-cloth" (2.5.13–14). Jonson's lists, unlike Shakespeare's, reflect a cluttered, irredeemable urban sprawl so overcrowded with things that it has become almost impossible for people to walk about naturally, a place where (in Hopkins's words) "all is seared with trade; bleared, smeared with toil, / And wears man's smudge, and shares man's smell" ("God's Grandeur"). Shakespeare's catalogues may be more attractive, but Jonson's comment more closely on the world in which almost all of us have to live.

In *Volpone*, most of the characters who struggle through this welter of objects seem to be animated less by souls or natural affections than by a strange lust for material possessions. The world they yearn to inhabit is hard, brilliant and metallic, still cluttered, but one in which light rebounds sharply from "bright cecchines," diamonds and orient pearls, "cloth of gold," massy plate, a carbuncle so fiery that it might "put out both the eyes of our St. MARKE" (1.4.69, 3.7.194). There are no shadows in this Venice of the avaricious imagination, and little softening of light into colour. It is cold and glittering, full of the sterile fire of gold or jewels in the sun, a fire that dazzles but has no power to warm. Against this icy glare, which by its nature cannot alter or decay, Jonson poises something diametrically opposed—an overpowering sense of the softness and corruptibility of human flesh. Here, as with so much of *Volpone*, *Sejanus* had already pointed the way. In the earlier work, physical dismemberment was not just the thing that happens literally to Sejanus at the end, but a recurrent image throughout. Characters were impelled to fragment the human form in speaking of it, and in doing so they made an unconscious comment upon the incoherence and dissolution of the body politic in Rome. But dismemberment is by no means the only, or even the chief, indignity inflicted upon bodies in the play. Jonson allows Sejanus to suggest to the physician Eudemus a series of positively Swiftian enquiries about the urine and faeces of the various great ladies upon whom he attends. He takes an interest too in "physic" in the subsidiary sense of "cosmetics":

> Which lady sleepes with her owne face, a nights?
> Which puts her teeth off, with her clothes, in court?
> Or, which her hayre? which her complexion?
> And, in which boxe she puts it?
>
> (1.307–10)

Left alone with Livia, his patient, Eudemus chatters on about ceruse, white oil, dentifrices, prepared pomatum, perfumes to induce a sweat, laxatives and medicinal baths, all the while touching up her features as though she were an image, not a living woman. Certainly her face is not her own.

On Capri, Tiberius is said to have erected a "slaughter-house . . . Where he doth studie murder, as an arte" (4.388–89), discovering which tortures will cause the most prolonged and excruciating pain. He is captivated too by sexual abnormality. Capri is stocked with beautiful boys and girls from the noblest Roman families, some persuaded to go there of their own free will, others brutally kidnapped, all handed over to the emperor's band of highly trained male prostitutes: "Masters of strange, and new-commented lusts, / For which wise nature hath not left a name" (4.400–401). Sejanus himself has risen to power by exploiting a corrupt sexuality. Arruntius remembers him as a serving boy, "when for hyre, / He prostituted his abused body / To that great gourmond, fat APICIUS; / And was the noted *pathick* of the time" (1.213–16). At the end, in a scene Tiberius himself might have been tempted to leave Capri to enjoy, Sejanus's virgin daughter, a mere child, is raped by the hangman before being strangled. Her mother Apicata, coming upon the corpses of the girl and her small brother, rends her own hair and flesh. The fact that these atrocities are only reported in the play, not seen, does not prevent them from generating an extraordinary atmosphere of physical horror. It seems appropriate in this place that poison, the slow destruction of the body from within, should be the favoured means for getting rid of men like Germanicus and Drusus, against whom Sejanus cannot proceed openly. As it does that Tiberius's face should be covered with pustules and eruptions ("ulcerous, and anointed," 4.174), imperfectly concealed by the application of viscous salves. In the final Senate scene, the gout, dropsy and "obsequious fatnesse" (ll. 455–60) of many of the Romans who attend make it difficult for them to shift themselves out of the vicinity of the doomed Sejanus with expedition as the tenor of Tiberius's letter finally becomes clear (5.621–25).

Sejanus is a play which talks constantly about statues, the dignified, immutable public images which people set up themselves. In this context, Jonson's stress upon the ephemeral, yielding nature of actual human flesh becomes increasingly uncomfortable. *Volpone* seizes upon a similar contrast, and carries it to an even further extreme. Although the sickness of the Fox is only feigned, it produces an astonishing collection of images of withering and putrefaction, rotting and physical decay. The old age of Corbaccio contributes more of them, as does the sexual obsessiveness of Corvino. Even Celia finds it easy to imagine the terrible disfigurements, leprosies and flayings which she would endure rather than yield to Volpone's lust. As Scoto of Mantua, Volpone harps on all the ills that flesh is heir to: catarrh, vomiting of blood, vertigo, cramps, convulsions, paralysis, epilepsy, vapours of the spleen and stoppings of the liver, the stone, strangury, dysentery, torsion of the small gut. Deformity can be forced upon the human body exceptionally by the accidents of birth or fortune, as in the case of the dwarf, the hermaphrodite and the eunuch. But even the most healthy and perfectly shaped are dying animals, vulnerable to disease and the processes of ageing. That man should be fixated on what is most alien and opposite to his mortal nature—cold, hard metals which cannot sicken or fade—represents a monstrous joke. Yet apart from Celia, Bonario and to some extent Peregrine and Sir Politic, it is a joke which can be made at the expense of every character in the play.

Jonson's "son" Robert Herrick, a poet steeped in Jonsonian attitudes and ways of handling language, managed to encapsulate the paradox upon which *Volpone* is built within a single, brilliant lyric, "To Dianeme":

> Sweet, be not proud of those two eyes,
> Which Star-like sparkle in their skies:
> Nor be you proud, that you can see

All hearts your captives; yours, yet free:
Be you not proud of that rich haire,
Which wantons with the Love-sick aire:
When as that *Rubie*, which you weare,
Sunk from the tip of your soft eare,
Will last to be a precious Stone,
When all your world of Beautie's gone.

Herrick's juxtaposition of the word "soft," at first sight flattering, with the indestructible "*Rubie*" is alarming in ways that abruptly rob the verb "Sunk" of its innocence. This kind of collision between deliquescing flesh and the hard, inanimate gems and gold it so incomprehensibly lusts to acquire informs *Volpone* throughout, contributing to a unity, a singleness of impression, that is new in Jonson's dramatic work. It can be said of this play, as of none he had written before, that it has the compactness and control of a lyric poem.

Vetus comoedia seems to have been a term which Jonson understood variously. When talking to Drummond about *The Devil Is an Ass*, he used it to pinpoint the play's indebtedness to the "old comedy" of England, the native morality tradition. Cordatus, on the other hand, clearly has Aristophanes in mind in the Induction to *Every Man out of His Humour*, when he claims that Asper's play is "strange, and of a particular kind by it selfe, somewhat like *Vetus Comoedia*." In fact, *Every Man out of His Humour* does not seem especially Aristophanic, except in so far as it is satiric, "neere, and familiarly allied to the time" (3.6.200–201), and probably contains a few unflattering portraits of contemporaries to whom Jonson had taken a dislike. Its Chorus is wholly unlike those of Aristophanes, and there are no structural resemblances. *Every Man out of His Humour* is indeed "of a particular kind by it selfe." With *Volpone*, however, the situation is different. There, the influence of Aristophanes is central and shaping.

The exact contents and extent of Jonson's library—or libraries—are now extremely difficult to ascertain. Much was destroyed in the fire of 1623. Jonson was also accustomed to sell his books periodically, whenever he ran short of money. It is clear, however, that at some stage he owned a copy of Aristophanes' plays. There is an edition (Geneva, 1607) in the Fitzwilliam Museum, Cambridge, which once belonged to the poet. He may well have owned others, now lost or impossible to trace to him. As Camden's pupil, and also as a man naturally interested in the comedy of the ancient world, both Roman and Greek, Jonson must have been acquainted with what survives of Athenian *vetus comoedia* long before he addressed himself to *Volpone*. But is was not until 1606 that he seems to have discovered Aristophanes creatively, understanding how this great dramatist might provide for him what Greek New Comedy had given most of his dramatic contemporaries, including Shakespeare: a basic comedic structure capable of subtle variation and extension.

In most of the extant plays of Aristophanes, a character or small group of characters conceives an improbable and extravagant idea: making a one-man peace treaty with Sparta, flying to heaven on the back of a gigantic dung-beetle, putting an end to international wars through sexual blackmail, enlisting the help of the birds to build a brick-walled city in the middle of the air and starve the gods into submission, bringing back a long-dead tragic poet from the underworld to save Athens from itself, or restoring the eyesight of the blind god of Wealth. The individuals who concoct these apparently lunatic schemes are usually self-seeking and rather suspect. Although the society against which they react, and which their scheme intends to subvert, is corrupt and foolish, Aristophanes refuses to make Dikaeopolis, Lysistrata, Trygaeus, Peithetairos or Euelpides into exemplary figures. They are comic rogues, whose own idea of what constitutes a comfortable and desirable life happens to conflict with the self-destructive impulses of the community in which they live. This is one reason why critical work on Aristophanes, as on the Jacobean Jonson, has been so bedevilled with disagreement as to the moral valency of the plays. The characteristic movement of Aristophanic comedy is towards the realization, against seemingly impossible odds, of a fantastic proposal. When this proposal has become fact, Aristophanes celebrates its establishment in a *komos*, and the comedy ends.

Both *The Case Is Altered* and *Every Man in His Humour* had borne witness to Jonson's uneasiness with the kind of linear, boy-gets-girl plot inherited from Greek New Comedy, the plot which for other Elizabethan dramatists was staple. The comical satires to which he turned next at least abandoned any pretence to interest in changeling children, resurrections from the dead, or romantic love leading to marriage. Yet "words, above action: matter, above words" had turned out to be an unsatisfactory substitute, especially in performance. Jonson had not been really successful in *Every Man out of His Humour, Cynthia's Revels* or *Poetaster* at replacing the well-tried organizational principles of contemporary comedy with any effective dramatic, as opposed to literary, structure. From this impasse he was rescued by Aristophanes. Aristophanic comedy was naturally congenial to him on a number of grounds. It was essentially urban, concerned to mirror the society in which its audience habitually lived, full of engaging scoundrels, frank—indeed, unabashedly scatological—in its handling of the body, concerned to merge the human with the animal world, frequently grotesque, unromantic yet poetic, a brilliant amalgam of realism and wild invention, and given to bestowing upon its characters significant, but not narrowly moral, names. Above all, it could provide Jonson with a structural alternative to the comic form favoured by his contemporaries that was theatrically workable and alive.

Volpone, The Silent Woman and *The Alchemist* are all plays which centre upon a fantastic and seemingly untenable idea. In *Volpone*, Jonson accepted some help from a familiar item of fox lore. The emblem of the fox "Stretch'd on the earth, with fine delusive sleights, / Mocking a gaping crow" (1.2.94–96) lies at the heart of the play. But its plot is basically Aristophanic: a triumphant demonstration that it is possible for one clever and self-interested rogue, with the help of an accomplice, to live off society's greed, amassing a vast private fortune simply by pretending to be terminally ill and uncertain as to the choice of an heir. This apparently far-fetched scheme is not only proved feasible—there is no practical reason it should not continue to flourish. Mosca makes a terrible mistake in act 3 when he fails to entertain the possibility that Bonario may leave the gallery where he was told to walk and read, and so become a witness not ony to Volpone's attempt to rape Celia, but to the fact that the invalidism of the Fox is all a cheat. Yet the miscalculation, as Jonson is at pains to show, is easily redeemed. Thanks to their own wit and effrontery, the greed of Voltore, Corbaccio and Corvino, the feebleness of wronged innocence, and the stupidity of the magistrates, Volpone and Mosca escape scot-free from a potentially deadly situation. The second scene of act 5 returns the Fox and the Fly, in effect, to the beginning of the comedy. Mosca can congratulate his patron and himself on regaining the safety of square one on the board:

> How now, sir? do's the day looke cleare againe?
> Are we recover'd? and wrought out of error,
> Into our way? to see our path, before us?
> Is our trade free, once more?
>
> (5.2.1–4)

"Yes" is the answer to every one of these rhetorical questions. Nothing, in fact, has changed after four long acts except that Volpone is even richer than he was, Corvino's marital dignity is now a little besmirched, and Celia and Bonario, both blameless victims, languish under a false accusation. It is astonishing, even to Mosca and Volpone, that the gulls cannot penetrate to the truth of their situation:

> they will not see't.
> Too much light blinds 'hem, I thinke. Each of 'hem
> Is so possest, and stuft with his owne hopes,
> That any thing, unto the contrary,
> Never so true, or never so apparent,
> Never so palpable, they will resist it.
>
> (5.2.22–27)

There is a desperate side to such lack of awareness, a stubborn refusal to understand that is bound up not only with greed, but with personal and imperfectly comprehended fears. When Mosca declares, "Here, we must rest; this is our master-peece:/We cannot thinke, to goe beyond this" (5.2.13–14), he is announcing the end of the comedy, its Aristophanic point of victory and celebration. Jonson, however, turns away from the *komos*. Instead of confirming the achievement of the Fox and the Fly, he goes on to explode it. But he makes it clear that this second ending is accidental, something which might have been almost indefinitely postponed.

Despite his intelligence and ironic ability to analyse and condemn vice in other people, Volpone partakes of the common self-ignorance. Because he never formulates his dangerous longing to break out of that enclosed, immobile existence in which his pretence is inviolable, he has little chance of mastering that longing. Jonson leaves the audience to draw its own conclusions as to just why Mosca chooses to tell Volpone about Corvino's wife, "The blaziang starre of *Italie*," and to do so in terms calculated to appeal both to his patron's sensuality and to his other dominating passion: "flesh, that melteth, in the touch, to bloud!/Bright as your gold! and lovely, as your gold!" (1.5.108, 113–14). Celia is introduced into the conversation abruptly, even awkwardly, merely because she happens to be beautiful and Lady Would-be, the next visitor in Volpone's timetable, is not. If Mosca intends here to tempt his master, he is entirely successful. The Fox passes immediately from the enquiry "Why had not I knowne this before?" (1.5.115) to a resolve to see this paragon himself, in some disguise. His performance as a mountebank, under Celia's window, earns him a thrashing from the outraged Corvino—the first physical pain that Volpone does not need to simulate in the play—but the real damage is to his sense of satisfaction with the life he leads. Celia's charms may be considerable, but the extreme nature of Volpone's response ("I cannot live, except thou helpe me, MOSCA," and "would thou/Had'st never told me of her," 2.4.8, 12–13) suggests that she is really the catalyst for a nebulous ennui which has slowly been accumulating over the three years of Volpone's self-imprisonment. There are drawbacks to the form of existence he has invented not mentioned in the encomiastic speeches of the first scene. Volpone can do nothing to prevent dreadful women like Lady Would-be from sitting by his bed for hours, boring him to distraction. Confinement, sexual abstinence and a routine enlivened only by contemplation of his treasure, food and drink, and the diversions provided by the eunuch, the hermaphrodite and the dwarf, cannot content a man of Volpone's vitality and imagination forever. Mosca is admirably placed to perceive that this is so. It seems likely that Volpone's extravagant offer to his parasite after he has become obsessed with Celia—

> take my keyes,
> Gold, plate, and jewells, all's at thy devotion;
> Employ them, how thou wilt; nay, coyne me, too:
> So thou, in this, but crowne my longings—
> (2.4.21–24)

although not meant literally, nonetheless represents the beginning of a shift of power in this relationship for which Mosca has successfully angled.

John Creaser writes persuasively about Volpone's shocked realization of his own impotence and fear after being carried into court in act 4. The fact that this time he and Mosca successfully evade exposure cannot conceal the narrowness of the escape, or the fact that in his alarm the Fox actually began to experience some of the physical symptoms—cramp and palsy—feigned for so long (5.1.1–17). Volpone's reckless insistence upon spreading the news of his death, installing Mosca as heir, and walking abroad in the habit of a Commendadore to taunt his disappointed victims, is indeed an attempt to regain ascendancy and control. Had he truly known Mosca, he would never have risked it, any more than even a superficial understanding of Celia would have allowed him to assume that she could be "collected" as unresistingly as a diamond, or a piece of embossed plate. Equally important, however, is the fact that although both previous ventures out of his lair into the liberty of the world outside have been fraught with peril, a newly restive and dissatisfied Fox cannot now remain indoors. The error, this time, is irrecoverable.

When all the truth is out, one of the Avocatori opines sententiously that "Mischiefes feed / Like beasts, till they be fat, and then they bleed" (5.12.150–51). The remark points usefully to the oddly fortuitous nature of this catastrophe—something which resembles the breaking of an impostume or internal tumour more than the healthy reassertion of a temporarily violated social order. Left to their own devices, the Avocatori would have expended their energies in competing for Mosca as a son-in-law. Villainy, locked in a secret, internecine struggle with itself, is forced to stand up and make a declaration of the facts before justice can be persuaded to take any notice. Mosca too has made a fatal miscalculation. He did not imagine that his patron, rather than make good that earlier rash offer of all his substance, "keyes, / Gold, plate, and jewells," would prefer to destroy both his accomplice and himself.

The sentences themselves, in which the punishments exquisitely fit the crimes, are unashamedly those of the dramatist rather than the obtuse magistrates of Venice. Sir Politic Would-be has already been condemned through the misdirected malice of Peregrine, and without the need of judicial process, to the condition he has expended so much energy trying to escape: that of a dull, ordinary Englishman abroad, distinguished by no knowledge of state secrets or special expertise. He has no choice now but to creep away, shrinking his poor head in his politic shell (5.4.88–89). For the others too, nemesis comes upon them in the shape of the thing each has most strenuously sought to avoid. Mosca, the parasite who has shunned the idea of actually working for a living, and for whom mobility, the freedom to "Shoot through the aire, as nimbly as a starre; / Turne short, as doth a swallow; and be here, / And there, and here, and yonder, all at once" (3.1.25–27) has been a precious prerogative, is condemned to hard labour and physical constriction, chained to a bench between the decks of a galley. The advocate Voltore, by contrast, whose legal skills have been the centre of his life and pride, is disbarred and forbidden ever to practise again. Corvino, whose terror of public disgrace has been almost pathological, is despatched on a ceremonial progress through Venice as an object of mockery, while Corbaccio, whose conviction that he would outlive Volpone, and that he was lusty yet despite the progressive failure of all five senses, is enclosed in the monastery of San Spirito, where he will be "learn'd to die" (5.12.133). Volpone himself, whose apprehension of real, as opposed to sham, physical pain precipitated him into the calamitous mistake of allowing Mosca to pose as heir, is sent to a prison from which he can never emerge, to be "crampt with irons, / Till thou bee'st sicke, and lame indeed" (5.12.123–24).

Only Celia and Bonario escape. Bonario, despite his earlier extreme of reverence for "the authority of a father," yields to the judgement of the court and takes possession of all Corbaccio's estate even though the old man is (just) alive. Celia is sent home to her father with her dowry trebled. But despite this legal separation from Corvino, there is no suggestion that Bonario—or any other young man—will figure in her future. Jonson has avoided throughout doing what would have seemed only natural to most other dramatists of the period: establishing any emotional bond between these two which, in time, might ripen into love. Celia and Bonario are the only characters at the end of the comedy (apart from Peregrine, who is not present in the final scene) whose lives remain open and, to a large extent, undetermined. Yet Jonson turns away from them without interest to focus instead on what Volpone himself wittily calls the "mortifying of a FOXE" (5.12.125). Volpone is not, like Sejanus, rendered speechless by the enormity of the fate which has come upon him. He has chosen to pull the whole house of cards down on his head rather than see Mosca triumph, and his own public verdict of the fools and knaves (5.12.89–94) precedes that of the judges. His last words in court are an ingenious, if bitter, joke. Moreover, Jonson allows him to remain behind the others to speak the Epilogue. This Epilogue, an appeal for audience approval, always elicits the applause for which it asks. It has sometimes been argued that here, and with the Epilogue spoken by Face at the end of *The Alchemist*, Jonson intends to trick audiences into a complicity with the villain which is really an indictment of their own corrupt tastes and reactions. But this is not morality drama. The Epilogue to *Volpone* is there to remind us that there are fictive criteria for judging scoundrels, older and more universal than the severities of Venetian law. Volpone cannot be forgiven within the play. No Justice Clement will pardon him, like Brainworm, "for the wit o'the offence." But the Fox, like Face, can rely on the spectators to acquit him of any crime committed against the spirit of comedy, for having been predictable, unimaginative or tedious. Here, as with all great comic heroes, from Dikaeopolis and Peithetairos to Falstaff, Autolycus or Marston's Cocledemoy, our indulgence justly sets him free.

The Play of Conspiracies in *Volpone*

William W. E. Slights

In 1980 at Oxford, Nigel Levaillant played Volpone with his legs in that unnaturally turned-out position characteristic of tightrope walkers, ballet dancers, and swordsmen. He tilted his head just so, as though posing for a vaguely inspirational portrait, and he caressed certain strategically placed words in Jonson's blank verse lines with richly operatic tones. I mean he *hammed* his way—stylishly, successfully—through the first four acts. And he took his cue for theatricality directly from Jonson's text:

> What should I doe
> But cocker vp my *genius* . . . ?
> (1.1.70–71)

> Now, my fain'd cough, my phthisick, and my gout,
> My apoplexie, palsie, and catarrhes,
> Helpe, with your forced functions, this my posture,
> Wherein, this three yeere, I haue milk'd their hopes.
> (1.2.124–27)

> But, were they gull'd
> With a beliefe, that I was SCOTO? MOSCA: Sir.
> SCOTO himselfe could hardly haue distinguish'd!
> (2.4.34–36)

From *Texas Studies in Literature and Language* 27, no. 4 (Winter 1985). © 1985 by the University of Texas Press.

> I am, now, as fresh,
> As hot, as high, and in as iouiall plight,
> As when (in that so celebrated *scene,*
> At recitation of our *comoedie,*
> For entertainment of the great VALOYS)
> I acted young ANTINOVS; and attracted
> The eyes, and eares of all the ladies, present,
> T'admire each gracefull gesture, note, and footing.
> (3.7.157–64)

If there was one thing that Volpone and Levaillant enjoyed doing, it was performing. So exclusive was their absorption in acting that one felt right from the start that, while histrionics was the actor's bread and butter, it would be the Magnifico's undoing. Given enough time, Volpone would, and did, upstage himself.

But Volpone's theatrical genius has perhaps been overstated in the critical literature and in production. In fact, the character-actor analogy is somewhat inaccurate because the success of Volpone's performance depends on his *not* being recognized as a performer by the other characters. Furthermore, *all* the charcters, not just Volpone, disguise their true desires and intentions in their attempts to control others. The real crux of the matter, then, is not Volpone's theatricality but the largely unquestioned assumption that men and women in the world of this play will pursue their own goals in secret. Secrecy is the societally condoned habit of mind that intensifies greed, lust, affectation, and mistrust. The dramatic mimesis of secrecy in *Volpone* is conspiracy, in which a small group schemes together secretly to deceive the rest of society. In each conspiracy Jonson uses techniques of the theater—disguise, plotting, and suspense—to comment satirically on those hidden forms of social intercourse invented and perpetuated by people for self-serving ends. In place of a shared community of interests, *Volpone* postulates a rivalry of conflicting ones, pursued through fraudulent shows of mutual concern. An interlocking set of conspiracies creates a distinctive pattern of personality and plot in *Volpone,* the primary function of which is to expose the folly of humanity's living together in a community devoid of mutual trust, respect, and openness.

Volpone's deceptions are normative in the fictional world of Venice, a world that not only tolerates but richly rewards secrecy. Mosca is constantly acting in collusion with others, occasionally with three or four factions at once. The three *captatores* (legacy hunters) feign devotion to the "sick" Volpone and offer him restoratives prepared to kill him. We can never be quite sure who Volpone's three freaks are: they have no clear-cut identities apart from the roles they play in the embedded fable of metempsychosis. Even Bonario and Celia have their public faces of pristine innocence while offering, in one case to spy on his father, in the other to prevaricate in collaboration with Volpone. The four *avocatori* appear to be seeking justice even as they try to forge alliances with Mosca sotto voce. The entire collection of secondary characters constitutes a society that perverts privacy into secrecy, theatrical flair into cynical conspiracy. The aside, the secret strategy session, and the whispered suspicion of plots and counterplots set a tone of uneasiness, of dis-ease in the play.

I propose to consider in this essay, first, the inclination toward secrecy in Jonson's London immediately preceding the first performance of *Volpone;* second, the specific theatrical strategies based on conspiracy that he built into the play; and, third, the two modes of discovering conspiracy—one false, one true,—that he employed to end his comedy. Studying the ways in which these conspiracies involve everyone in the play should, finally, help us to see how Jonson's satire can coopt, comically diminish, and hence discredit the bias toward secrecy in a culture nearly paralyzed by its collective anxiety.

Without relying too heavily on biographical information, which is at best incomplete, at worst a reflection of Jonson's conscious attempts to cut a controversial figure. I believe that we can see in *Volpone* something of Jonson's own frustrations in a world that conducts its business under a veil of secrecy. The play, better known throughout the seventeeth century by its running title, *The Foxe,* was composed and played in the immediate wake of the plot to blow up Parliament, which was engineered unsuccessfully in 1605 by Guy Fawkes, the man whose name was to live in Enlgish history as a synonym for stealth and treachery. Whether or not the Fawkes-Fox pun was intended to signal the topicality of Jonson's satire, there can be little doubt that conspiracy was an issue of high interest at the time. The hunt for Jesuit sympathizers created particularly treacherous undercurrents in London, and Jonson, a well-known Catholic recusant, was called upon by the Privy Council to contact a priest wanted for questioning in connection with the Gunpowder incident. Counterplots and accusations were rife. Typical of the scare-literature being written at the time is William Leigh's *Great Britains great deliverance from popish powder,* entered in the Stationer's Register in January 1606. With clear hindsight Leigh bereates Englishmen for having ignored their sacred duty to remain vigilant in spying out papists:

> We should have seene these miscreants, neuer sated with the
> bloud of the Saints, til they had changed our religion for su-
> perstition, our knowledge for ignorance, our preaching for

massing; our subjects for Rebels, our Counsellors for conspirators, and so haue brought vpon vs, and ours: A most wofull
Sabaoth, when both the lawes of God & man (which are the
sinewes of a sanctified state) had beene dissolued, and silent.

There is a hint of the satirist's reforming zeal in Leigh's catalog of Roman
ambitions, but more of the government official's readiness to find a papist
under every Protestant bed, as appears clearly in his subsequent appeal to
English fears: "Againe, take heed of them, for they are busie bodies, and
walke inordinately amongst you: they are impatient of our possession, great
peace, and much plentie."

We might also note here that although busybodies of whatever per-
suasion were often targets of scorn in Jonson's comedies and epigrams, he
would certainly not have subscribed to William Leigh's solution that "I will
fight against you with your owne weapons, and I will weary you in your
owne waies." Jonson's abhorence of this kind of doing unto others, fighting
secrecy with secrecy, goes some way toward explaining the pattern of
personality and plotting in *Volpone*. Jonson had been personally harassed
by government informers while in prison, and he was cited for recusancy
before the Consistory Court of London on January 10, 1605/06:

Presented, that they [Jonson and his wife] refuse not to Come
to divyne servis but have absented them selves from the
Co[mmun]ion beinge oftentymes admonished w[hi]ch hathe
Continued as farr as we Can learne ever since the kinge Came
in[.] he is a poett and is by fame a seducer of youthe to ye popishe
Religion.

Given this kind of surveillance and interpretation of his private actions, it
is no wonder that Jonson mistrusted "politique *Picklocke[s]* of the *Scene*"
(*Bartholomew Fair*, Induction, l. 138), men who would search his public
utterances for subversive meanings.

Jonson's fellow poet, John Donne, likewise embraced Roman Ca-
tholicism and had, during the reign of the old queen, fashioned the world
of the frightened recusant into the stuff of satire. The speaker of Donne's
Satyre IV, pumped for his opinions by a chattering courtier of the Sir Pol
species, had felt "One of our Giant Statutes ope his jaw / To sucke me in"
(ll. 132–33) and, in the closing lines of the poem, admits that "I shooke
like a spyed Spie" (l. 237) quite without reason. Several characters in *Volpone*
eventually suffer the fate of the "spyed Spie" when Volpone himself reveals
their illegal, clandestine activities.

Although, as we shall see, Jonson had recognized the dramatic potential of conspiracy in tragedy well before the discovery of the Gunpowder Plot and the subsequent period of paranoia during which *Volpone* was written, the play marks the beginning of Jonson's penetrating analysis of the problems of his secrecy-ridden society on the comic stage. In the play, conspiracy takes the form of earnest financial fraud, medical quackery, courtroom perjury, and sexual assault, among others. While similar forms of violence and deceit occurred, for example, in Jonson's early plays based on Roman intrigue comedy, his understanding of the moral implications of conspiracy was different in his middle plays. He gives new meaning to "intrigue" comedy. In the early play, *Every Man in His Humour* (1598), for instance, Musco, like the conventional much abused slave of Roman comedy, bounces back irrepressibly with fresh schemes that the audience wishes to see succeed. As in the classical models, the servant in *Every Man In* usually works alone to achieve limited goals that help to foster a lighthearted complicity with the audience through his asides, soliloquies, and whatever winks, grins, and shrugs the actor can use to ingratiate himself with the audience.

In *Volpone,* by contrast, nearly everyone in the play has become his or her own Musco, and the trickster's alliance with the cause of young love has become at once vestigial and unsavory. The audience can no longer relax into a winking conspiracy. In the tinny casuistry of Corvino's pandering, the smug chuckle of Mosca's encomium on parasites (3.1.1–33), and the cynical gloating of the inventory scene (5.3), Jonson lets his audience hear the hollowness of laughter at human exploitation, however cleverly executed, and he shows us the moral maze of an easy complicity. Such pleasures of comedy, like laughter itself when divorced from judgment, are denied Jonson's audience. His comments on the subject of mindless laughter in *Discoveries,* as well as in the plays and prologues, are devastating: "the moving of laughter . . . is rather a fowling for the peoples delight, or their fooling. . . . this is truly leaping from the Stage to the Tumbrell againe, reducing all witt to the originall Dungcart" (*Disc.,*ll. 2629–30, 2675–77). This view of the abuses to which stage comedy was prone suggests why Jonson might have turned from the rather raucous humor of his comical satires *Cynthia's Revels* (1600) and *Poetaster* (1601) to the vicious ironies of *Sejanus* (1603), the first play in which he treated conspiracy as a tragic theme. Later, after treating the subject comically in *Volpone* (1606), *The Alchemist* (1610), and to a lesser extent in *Epicoene* (1609), he returned specifically to the fatal effects of conspiracy on the body politic in his tragedy, *Catiline His Conspiracy* (1611).

In order to trace the subtle play of conspiracy that I believe underlies the comic structure and moral vision of *Volpone,* I shall look closely at the dialogue in several brief episodes that shape audience expectations going into the play's climactic trial scenes. Each of these episodes incorporates not only the theatrical talents of the chief conspirators, Volpone and Mosca, but also definite hints of the debiliatating effects of conspiracy on all the charcters, especially on their family relationships.

Each meeting between Volpone and one of the spying *captatores* in the first act is preceded by private conversations, first between Mosca and his master, then between Mosca and the gull. The presentation of bribes to Volpone and the furious negotiation for assurances of the inheritance are extensions of the terms and motives worked out in the preceding private conspiracies. In the play's second scene, for example, Mosca announces to Volpone that Signior Voltore is waiting outside to see him. Master and servant then mock the legacy hunters for their animal rapaciousness, crude disguises, and gullibility:

> VOLPONE: Now, now, my clients
> Beginne their visitation! vulture, kite,
> Rauen, and gor-crow, all my birds of prey,
> That thinke me turning carcasse, now they come:
> I am not for 'hem yet.
>
> MOSCA: Hood an asse, with reuerend purple,
> So you can hide his two ambitious eares,
> And, he shall passe for a cathedrall Doctor.
> (1.2.87–113)

Mosca's caricature or Voltore as an ass disguised as a learned doctor of laws reveals that he is aware of other "fine delusiue sleights" (l. 95) abroad than the one he and Volpone are devising to cheat Voltore. The gull is himself a would-be conspirator. Acting on this awarness, Mosca pretends in the opening lines of the next scene to conspire with Voltore against Volpone and the rival captatores: "Onely you / (Of all the rest) are he, commands his loue" (1.3.1–2). Then, during the central section of the scene, Mosca plays confidant to Voltore and Volpone simultaneously:

> (MOSCA: You are his heire, sir.
> VOLTORE: Am I?) VOLPONE: I feele me going, (vh, vh,
> vh, vh.)
> I am sayling to my port, (vh, vh, vh, vh?)
> And I am glad, I am so neere my hauen.
> MOSCA: Alas, kind gentleman, well, we must all goe.
> (1.3.27–31)

While Mosca's asides to Voltore suggest conspiracy between them, his faithful echoing of Volpone's platitudes on the inevitability of death signal to the audience his deeper complicity with his master. As for Voltore, his efforts at conspiracy are totally self-defeating; he pretends with Mosca to be taken in by Volpone's cant, while in fact it is he who is being taken in.

The same pattern of entwined conspiracies is repeated in the interviews with Corbaccio and Corvino with even more chilling effect: first, Mosca schemes genuinely with Volpone (though always keeping his options open), then falsely with the visitor, and finally with both together. The effect is to place Mosca in the pivotal position of all character relationships, even while Volpone holds center stage in a series of plays within the play. Mosca even succeeds in inducing Bonario to eavesdrop on his father, much as Iago conspires with Othello against Cassio, though Mosca dare not promise ocular proof:

> if you
> Shall be but pleas'd to goe with me, I'le bring you,
> (I dare not say where you shall see, but) where
> Your eare shall be a witnesse of the deed;
> Heare your selfe written bastard: and profest
> The common issue of the earth.
>
> (3.2.60–65)

While Mosca is out of Volpone's house conspiring with Bonario, Lady Politic Would-be visits and easily dominates the unsupported Volpone. Only the servant's timely return keeps this significiant variation of the pattern of Volpone-Mosca preconspiracies from being a disaster. Mosca's solution to the problem is to send Lady Pol chasing off in search of yet another conspiracy, the alleged assignation between her husband and a Venetian courtesan. What she stumbles into on the Rialto is not the conspiracy she expected, but another one: her husband keeping close counsel with a counterfeit English spy, Peregrine, whom she mistakes for "A female deuill, in a male out-side" (4.2.56). Even this apparently inconsequential and totally misconstrued conspiracy will subsequently be turned to Volpone's hostile purposes in the first trial scene. Like the fanatical antipapist William Leigh, Lady Would-be imagines conspiracy to be lurking everywhere and is all too eager to testify against those she suspects. Her zeal to uncover intrigues and to share in Volpone's "possessions . . . and much plentie" only prevent her from seeing who the real conspirators are, however.

The purpose of conspiracy that emerges from the episodes I have reviewed so far is to outwit one's rivals by obscuring one's real motives.

The basic absurdity that renders these actions comic is that the instigator of conspiracy must employ the aid of another, or others, for two reasons: to gain credibility by generating an apparent consensus (i.e., the conspirator's tales assume the ring of truth by being repeated by his cohort) and to provide him an appreciative audience in an action that would otherwise lose the thrill of performance. The fundamental contradiction between reliance on a fellow conspirator and clandestine pursuit of a selfish prize becomes the central element of closure in Jonson's comedy, as we shall see. In the short run, however, conspiracy provides gratification and applause as well as release for the conspirators' hostility toward the rest of humanity.

Patterns of performance and conspiracy deepen and darken into the arrangements for a gruesome travesty of offering the gift of heavenly love (the merchant's wife is named Celia, the heavenly one) to the supposedly dying old lecher. The sequence begins as a conspiracy between Mosca and the merchant, Corvino. Mosca reports that his master has been temporarily revived by a dose of Scoto's oil and that the "colledge of physicians" (2.6.27) has now supposedly prescribed a young woman, "Lustie, and full of iuice," (l. 35) to restore Volpone's vitality. Corvino is particularly distressed to learn that a rival captatore, one Dr. Lupus, has already offered his daughter for the purpose. Mosca patiently nurtures the seed of an idea in his gull's mind: Corvino's wife will meet the requirements admirably, and the reluctant husband can rationalize away his moral scruples (actually his jealousy) if only he can convince himself that he will win the prize of Volpone's inheritance by pandering for his own wife. Playing the appreciative audience, a role he is much practiced in, Mosca waits for Corvino to unfold the plot, as if it were his "owne free motion" (l. 95), and applauds him enthusiastically for thinking of the very thing that Mosca himself would have suggested were he not reluctant to "seeme to counsell" Corvino (l. 82). Mosca has so artfully arranged the conspiracy to get Celia for his master that Corvino is satisfied that he himself is the source of a powerful idea, the distributor of benefits, and the certain winner of a still grander prize, yet to be awarded.

When Corvino all but shoves his wife into Volpone's bedchamber and then withdraws with Mosca (3.7), Volpone is abandoned, for the second time in the play, to his own devices, and things go just as badly as they had in the interview with Lady Pol. Having lost his chief conspirator, Mosca, he tries to cast Celia in that role, with disastrous results. He confides that it was he, Volpone, who appeared that very morning at her window in the shape of a mountebank. That masquerade having worked so successfully, he proposes that, together, they continue to baffle the jealous husband. He boasts that

> before
> I would haue left my practice, for thy loue,
> In varying figures, I would haue contended
> With the blue PROTEVS, or the horned *Floud.*
>
> (3.7.150–53)

Certainly Volpone's claims are a fitting extension of his past Protean performances, but this time he has conspired with someone who does not share his hostile delight in deception. His analogies between himself and Proteus and the river god Achelous, who fought in many shapes to win Dianeira, are utterly presumptuous, pride being not so much an isolated flaw as a basic axiom of Volpone's character. His attempt to replay the lusty young hero of an Ovidian entertainment, as in William Gager's university play, *Ulysses Redux* (1592), simply makes Volpone look awkward and foolish.

> I am, now, as fresh,
> As hot, as high, and in as iouiall plight,
> As when (in that so celebrated *scene,*
> At recitation of our *comoedie,*
> For entertainment of the great VALOYS)
> I acted young ANTINOVS; and attracted
> The eyes, and eares of all the ladies, present,
> T'admire each gracefull gesture, note, and footing.
>
> (3.7.157–64)

Celia retreats before his torrent of words and his fancy footwork; for Jonson's purposes she need do nothing more to encourage Volpone's tirade and to solidify the audience's impression of his folly.

Volpone continues his virtuoso performance with the famous carpe diem lyric adapted from Catullus ("*Come, my* CELIA, *let vs proue*"), charming in itself but devastating to his cause in this context. The middle section of the song, often ignored by interpreters of the play, extends Jonson's exploration of deceit, spying, and conspiracy into the arena of supposed lovers' "*wile*[s]."

> *Cannot we delude the eyes*
> *Of a few poore houshold-spies?*
> *Or his easier eares beguile,*
> *Thus remooued, by our wile?*
>
> (3.7.176–79)

The theme of the entire song is not love but the urge to "delude": first Time, the destroyer, then the jealous husband, and finally an entire society's system for spying out "crimes" (l. 183). The social divisiveness that Volpone advocates in the song, harmless enough in the context of Catullus's little book of verse but thoroughly nasty in Jonson's play, compounds itself ironically when the effect of the song is further to alienate the "beloved."

The more Celia "droopes" and prays for some calamity to end the assault, the more Volpone persists in building his vaguely nauseating word-worlds of inedible private banquets, finally setting the whole thing "whirl[ing] round / With the *vertigo*" (ll. 218–19). He imagines that while his dwarf, eunuch, and fool perform a dizzying dance,

> we, in changed shapes, [shall] act OVIDS tales,
> Thou, like EVROPA now, I like IOVE,
> Then I like MARS, and thou like ERYCINE,
> So, of the rest, till we haue quite run through
> And weary'd all the fables of the gods.
>
> (3.7.221–25)

Volpone's choice of mythological rapes as examples of romantic apotheosis reminds the audience of a sordid reality that Volpone seems totally to have forgotten. Try as she may, Celia can produce no arguments to deter Volpone from his high-flown imaginings. He sees her only as his partner in fable and conspiracy, and her demurs have no place in that script. Only inadvertently does she bring Volpone down with a jolt when she offers to report him virtuous, thereby actually offering to enter, on her own terms, his conspiracy to deceive the world. Volpone is flabbergasted: "Thinks me cold, / Frosen, and impotent, and so report me?" (ll. 260–61). Having thrown aside his mask of diseased incapacity at the beginning of the scene, the self-styled virtuoso in sexuality feels he must now at all costs establish his credentials as a lusty scoundrel. In a marvelously comic show of misplaced loyalty, he refuses to disgrace the reputation of all Italian lechers. Later he is to sweat profusely as he sits helplessly by in his invalid's chair at the *scrutineo* while his lawyer scorns the very notion of his sexual prowess. Are these palsied hands "fit to stroake a ladies brests?" demands the advocate; and when the trial is over, Volpone needs strong wine to steady those shaking hands and to dispel the heartsick humor that he is indeed past his prime. (4.6.27–28, 5.1.11–12). Confronted with Celia, he had to prove himself a virile villain, but for all his supposed erotic poetry, Volpone finds himself at the end of the seduction scene recoiling in horror from Celia's suggestion that she report him to suffer, as he puts it, from "NESTOR'S *hernia*," the classic sign of impotence (3.7.262). Before he can fully recover from his insult, the would-be ravisher is interrupted and routed by Bonario.

The effect of conspiracy in the seduction scene, as in the play generally, is to constrict projected and perceived personalities. The expansiveness we ordinarily associate with game- and role-playing is smothered in secrecy. If this is so, we may need to reevaluate the usual approach to Jonson's satiric comedy in the classroom and the theater, which is to attribute severely limited powers of perception to his gulls while largely crediting the extravagant claims of subtlety and imaginative freedom made by his tricksters. Such pronounced contrasts are easily taught and easily staged: the deaf and dottering Corbaccio could, in this view, no more initiate a master plot than the supple, ubiquitous Mosca could fail to do so. The parasite's praise of "elegant" parasites is ordinarily taken as a fair description of his own modus operandi in the play:

> your fine, elegant rascall . . . can rise,
> And stoope (almost together) like an arrow;
> Shoot through the aire, as nimbly as a starre;
> Turne short, as doth a swallow; and be here,
> And there, and here, and yonder, all at once;
> Present to any humour, all occasion;
> And change a visor, swifter, then a thought!
>
> (3.1.23–29)

But Jonson gives this supposed meteor among men only one such vital soliloquy in the entire play. Much of the time, Mosca takes his cues from the gulls with whom he is conspiring, and they are nearly always cues for banality, as we noticed in his platitudinizing about death (1.3). He has none of the vision of a Sir Epicure Mammon, and his plots seem paltry next to those of Marlowe's Barabas, neither of whom suffers the psychological constriction that Jonson here attributes to the conspiring habit of mind.

Jonson dramatizes this psychological restriction still more fully in the case of Volpone, who, like Mosca, claims freedom from all constraining ties, though he can do so only in negative terms, even in his famous opening speeches:

> I blow no subtill glasse; expose no ships
> To threatenings of the furrow-faced sea;
> I turne no moneys, in the publike banke;
> Nor vsure priuate—
>
> (1.1.37–40)

> I haue no wife, no parent, child, allie,
> To giue my substance to.
>
> (1.1.73–74)

With no significant economic activity or personal relationships to engage him, Volpone resorts to playing dress-up. His disguises move him downward on the social scale from Magnifico to mountebank to courtroom flunky, and downward on a scale of vitality from robust schemer to palsy-shaken old man to corpse. A further concrete image of the limits of his mind is the severe restriction of his bodily movements: he has, not a kingdom, but a bedroom for a stage, and when he tries to extend his theatrical conspiracy beyond those four walls, he experiences genuine terror, as in the wake of the first trial scene:

> I ne're was in dislike with my disguise,
> Till this fled moment; here, t'was good, in priuate,
> But in your publike, *Caue,* whil'st I breathe.
>
> (5.1.2–4)

Later he confesses that a "dull deuill . . . in this braine of mine" has caused him to relinquish his power unwittingly to his servant (5.11.4–5). Nothing will do but he must indulge his "conceipts," "crotchets," and "*conundrums*" (5.11.13–17). Each of these terms, taken from his speech of self-chastizement, stresses the intellectual pettiness and whimsicality of Volpone's enterprise. Like the villainies of Macbeth, Volpone's contemporary on the tragic stage, Volpone's actions and modes of thought tend to diminish rather than to enlarge or ennoble him.

The blighting of sexuality and the comic deflation of the main character are two of the directly observable consequences of the conspiring habit of mind in *Volpone.* We have also seen the disturbing effects of conspiracy on the bonds between father and son (Bonario and Corbaccio) as well as husband and wife (Corvino and Celia). To this list we can add Lady Pol's unconscious travesty of humanist learning as she uses books and ideas as tokens to gain entrance into what she imagines to be the closed circle of the Venetian intelligentsia. Similarly Sir Pol's fascination with the latest gossip about London's secret agents leads him to view life as an extended game of clever mechanical devices. While the discovery and mocking of Sir Pol's "secrets" can be achieved by a simple, farcical unmasking action in the subplot, unraveling the serious consequences of conspiracy in the main plot involves Jonson and his audience in more elaborate indirections.

Bonario's intervention during the seduction scene proves to be one

step, but a false one, in the process of discovery. He foils Volpone's seduction attempt at the last minute, commanding him, "Forebeare, foule
rauisher, libidinous swine, / Free the forc'd lady" (3.7.267–68). The diction
and cadence of his speeches, borrowed from heroic romance, provide one
final humorous touch in the scene. Like the lyricism of Catullus and the
eroticism of Ovid, the heroism of Spenser's Red-Crosse Knight is ridiculously out of place in Volpone's bedroom. The dashing lone hero has no
serious answers for this society where everyone lurks in dark corners and
no one much regards the law. Even the denouncer of foul ravishers has
turned spy in a way that breeches the "bond . . . 'twixt son and father" as
surely as does the more famous action of the contemporary play, *King Lear*.
The collapse of social bonds and contracts under the pressure of conspiracy
is given special ironic force in *Volpone* as well as *King Lear* by the inclusion
of formal trial scenes.

Volpone and his allies are brought to trial twice in the course of the
action, the first time immediately following the abortive seduction scene.
Jonson had used trial scenes in his comical satires as a way to present in
orderly fashion key issues such as courtly pretension (*Cynthia's Revels*) and
false art (*Poetaster*). In these plays spokesmen for justice passed judgment
and assigned punishments. The courtroom scenes in *Volpone* serve a different
purpose, however. In these scenes the central issue of conspiracy is dra-
matized, not merely commented on. The courts and pseudocourts of Jonson's middle comedies are hardly models of the orderly dispensation of
justice. What strikes the *avocatori* in *Volpone* as a temporary procedural
problem—lack of order in the courtroom and of clarity in the proceedings—
in fact mirrors and even ratifies the violation of familial, sexual, and financial
bonds in the first three acts. In the course of the second trial one perplexed
judge exclaims, "This same's a labyrinth!" and another echoes the sentiment, saying, "This is confusion" (5.10.42, 47). The point of this con-
sternation is not simply the judges' obtuseness but the ease with which a
community given to secrecy can be divided against itself. The well-spring
of the confusion is, as always in Jonson, the human tongue divorced from
truth and reality. To be persuasive in a world such as Volpone's Venice,
the fast-talker need only slightly skew one basic premise of rhetoric—that
speech should be adjusted to suit the particular audience—by spinning out
a different tale for each faction of hearers. The inventive deceits of such
speakers will not be confined by the bond of any oath administered in the
courts.

The professional tongue-wager in the courtooom is Voltore, Volpone's
lawyer and aspirant to his inheritance. Early in act 1 Mosca marvels that

Voltore is a man "of so perplex'd a tongue, / And loud withall, that would not wag, nor scarce / Lie still, without a fee" (1.3.63–65), and after the first trial he enthusiastically tells Voltore that his "tongue [should be] tipt with gold" (4.6.64). Though Mosca's remarks are pure flattery, he also believes that under the circumstances words are golden; that is without Voltore to orchestrate the conspirators, the fortune might have been lost. Yet Mosca also knows that the words of the golden-tongued lawyer are nothing but useful noise, a kind of verbal chaos that obscures for the moment the knavery of Volpone. "We will but vse his tongue, his noise," Mosca tells Corvino (4.4.11). As with Volpone's masterful obfuscation in the mountebank scene, Voltore's speeches in the present instance flow into the realm of insubstantial jargon. He asserts, with Corvino's nodded consent, that the wronged husband knew of a sexual liaison between Celia and Bonario; he then goes on to bereate the young couple for presuming further on the willing cuckold's mercy:

> For these, not knowing how to owe a gift
> Of that deare grace, but with their shame; being plac'd
> So' aboue all powers of their gratitude,
> Began to hate the benefit; and, in place
> Of thankes, deuise t' extirpe the memorie
> Of such an act. Wherein, I pray your father-hoods,
> To obserue the malice, yea, the rage of creatures
> Discouer'd in their euils; and what heart
> Such take, euen, from their crimes.
>
> (4.5.44–52)

The functional words in the speech are a series of nouns—"shame," "malice," "rage," "euils," "crimes." The only "crime" named in the speech, however, is ingratitude for the rather dubious favor that has become in Voltore's account no less than a gift of grace. The richly emotive language of prosecution obscures what is really going on just as surely as Volpone's early promises of profit and declaration of love had done.

However prominent and pyrotechnical the advocate's art of obfuscation might be, the chilling fact remains that little ingenuity is required beyond a conspiracy of witnesses to make a mockery of innocence and judicial proceedings. Bonario and Cleia place their entire trust in God and the law. Of course, they appear foolish to do so in the present circumstance, for it is the nature of the Fox and his cohorts to turn witty imposture against established communal authority. False testimonies from Celia's husband and Lady Would-be, and Volpone's masquerade in the invalid's chair, plausibly make the accusing parties appear to the court as the accused, indeed the guilty parties. The legal monster of Donn's *Satyre IV,* who thrives only through the bad offices of spies and informers, is prepared to "ope his jaw / To sucke . . . in" the play's young innocents. Bonario and Celia revert to ridiculously hollow special pleadings that the avocatori consider "no testimonies" at all (4.6.18). These judges may have already revealed their dullness and will subsequently show their venality, but what member of Jonson's audience could have arrived at a different verdict after hearing only the evidence presented in the first trial? The plot seems to have come to a cynical and wholly repugnant conclusion, leaving Volpone to savor his successful upending of justice. Apparently Jonson has thrown Bonario's and Celia's "unworldliness into the arena: hers to be mauled by the wolves, his to be applauded by the asses," as one critic says, thus extending the beast fable to include the audience's inhuman reactions. But has he discarded his foolish innocents cynically, or has he rather used them to demonstrate how easily justice may be subverted by craft and to force his audience to reject this inadequate ending to his comedy? If so in rejecting the morally downbeat ending, we presumably reject all that it implies about the glamour of the trickster's life and the advantages of secrecy. Giving the audience what it may have thought it wanted in the triumph of villainy, Jonson, in fact, causes us to reject a cheap, conspiratorial victory in favor of another ending yet to come.

To argue that Jonson establishes moral priorities by indulging the audience's secret desire for the Fox to escape punishment at the end of act 4 is not to say that we must expect from his comedy only lighthearted forms of closure, what Jonson elsewhere called *"the Concupiscence of Daunces, and Antickes."* Instead, Jonson has used the double ending of his comedy to probe the most distasteful sorts of human commerce, "to put the snaffle in [the] mouths" of Puritan theater critics with a vengeance (Epistle to *Volpone,* l. 115), and to make his viewers see more clearly the real values of communal living, including social hierarchy. To do this requires a further twist in the plot, the comic inversion of the master-servant relationship and a movement toward openness in people's dealings with one another.

Jonson revives his plot at the beginning of act 5 and prepares for an ending to its comic deceptions totally different from anything before seen on the English stage. We glimpse for a moment the chink in Volpone's armor: the trickster's abiding fear that the infinite variety of identities has found in his personal Pandora's box might vanish and the reality of a "dead palsey" put an end to life's masquerade:

> A many of these feares
> Would put me into some villanous disease,
> Should they come thick vpon me: I'le preuent 'hem.
> Giue me a boule of lustie wine, to fright
> This humor from my heart.
>
> (5.1.8–12)

Earlier, Volpone has floated above life on an insulating layer of disguise and material objects—much gold, some furs, "lustie wine," Turkish carpets, down beds—that were continually being cataloged, more to establish their volume than their value. There in the public courtroom in act 4, the insulation grew too thin for comfort, and the chill of fear replaced the heat of elation. Mosca, seeing his chance, cleverly mocks and feeds the fear ("But confesse, sir, / Were you not daunted?" [5.2.38–39]) until Volpone feels himself constrained to overreach his past deceptions as a way to reasserting his faith in scheming. He volunteers to don the ultimate and ultimately terrifying disguise of death. He commands a pair of his cohorts,

> Go,
> Streight, giue out, about the streetes, you two,
> That I am dead; doe it with constancy,
> Sadly, doe you heare? impute it to the griefe
> Of this late slander
>
> . . . .
>
> I shall haue, instantly, my vulture, crow,
> Rauen, come flying hither (on the newes)
> To peck for carrion, my shee-wolf, and all,
> Greedy, and full of expectation.
>
> (5.2.59–67)

The injunction to "doe it with constancy" (i.e., to act consistently in character) reverberates ironically in context, since by making his servant, Mosca, his master, Volpone effectively destroys the shifting ground of his multiple conspiracies. He must remain permanently "dead." After all, while a dead man requires an executor of his will, the living no longer need the dead. Volpone has written himself out of the script, or rather, he may now speak *only* in asides or as another person—the ultimate trap of secrecy. The Fox will slip this trap, but only to be fixed with a final, until-death identity as a prisoner in chains.

The uncasing action of act 5 repeats many of the events of the earlier acts but with a significant variation: elaborate theatrical pretenses are renewed, but this time Volpone and Mosca abandon their practice of flattering and cajoling their dupes in favor of the more offensive tactic of gloating over the fools' disappointments. Like Peregrine stripping Sir Pol of his tortoise shell and then mocking his vulnerability in the subplot (5.2), first Mosca, enthusiastically assuming the role of Volpone's heir in the inventory scene (5.3), and then Volpone himself, disguised as an officer of the law (5.6–9), mock the foiled captatores. In the final trial scene Mosca holds his master's keys and title, indeed his very identity, publicly refusing to acknowledge his existence or to share the spoils of their confederacy. To the surprise of everyone on stage and in the audience, Volpone drops his disguise and calls down the law on the head of his upstart servant. This, Volpone's most desperate use of the Venetian legal system for his own purposes, is also his last, since it entails revealing the truth about his own deceptions as well. With the possibilities of further conspiracy exhausted, the play naturally comes to an end. The former conspirators are all stripped of their valuables and committed to various forms of incarceration and humiliation. As in the subplot's scene of exposure, with its tawdry tortoise shell retreat, Johnson gives mimetic life to the point that no one can escape the realities of his nature and his world by taking permanent refuge in theatrical artifice.

It has become fashionable, in the wake of Stanley Fish's affective reading of seventeenth-century texts, to argue that Jonson draws even his audience into a kind of conspiracy with his characters, only to surprise them with the sudden revelation that they too have sinned. Though it is certainly true that Jonson was willing to surprise his audience on occasion (viz., the ending of *Epicoene*) and to insult their critical intelligence (as in the Introduction to *Bartholomew Fair*), I am not convinced that the audience of *Volpone* is treated like this. The onstage audience—those applauding co-conspirators—*are* stung in precisely this way, but almost anyone watching Jonson's play unfold can reasonably be expected to remain at arm's length from the theatrical spectacle that so enraptures and then disillusions Jonson's characters. We have already seen this kind of aesthetic distance forced on the audience by the outcome of the first trial scene. Having been allowed backstage, so to speak, during the scenes of conspiracy to watch the preparation of scripts, costumes, and even makeup, we have been encouraged from the start to judge the actor's art with a critical eye. Far from glamorizing what Pico called "our chameleon," Jonson makes self-transforming conspiracy the chief butt of his satire.

In *Volpone* Jonson has made a comic form, based on the conspicuous contrivance of intrigue comedy, where schemes self-destruct because their designers have tried to play life as a conspiratorial game devoid of serious consequences. The game is highly amusing to watch unfold, deeply satisfying to see concluded. It is concluded by an inadvertent shift to openness in a society formerly compartmentalized by secrecy. The shift is caused not by the intervention of an influential, easygoing, wittily outspoken advocate of civic harmony such as Justice Clement but rather by internal pressures in the society that force characters and plots to exhaust the resources of secrecy. The techniques of theatrical discovery, including the act of unmasking and the virtual detheatricalizing of life as the play moves toward the moral conclusion of Volpone's epilogue, doubtless had, as they still have, a stinging relevance for an audience familiar with the antics of spies and informers. Both as Catholic recusant and as satirist, Jonson courageously, disdained the cautious advice of timid men like his would-be intriguer, Sir Pol:

> not [to] tell a secret,
> On any termes, not to your father; scarse
> A fable, but with caution; make sure choise
> Both of your company, and discourse; beware,
> You neuer speake a truth.
>
> (4.1.13–17)

The outcome of such secrecy, as Jonson set out to show in *Volpone,* is the total suppression of truth in matters of money, marriage, statecraft, and religion. Writing at a moment of acute political crisis in Jacobean England, immediately following the discovery of the Gunpowder Plot, Jonson implicitly attacked the conspiratorial excesses of both the counterrevolutionary Roman Catholic forces and the Protestant establishment. In so doing, he simultaneously managed to ridicule the false forms of theatricality that to his mind had infected the English stage and to create a comic form that remains "neere, and familiarly allied to the time" (*Every Man out of His Humour,* Grex, 3.6.200–201). Because the new form captured men in their most awkward public poses and at their most conspiratorial whisperings, Volpone swings madly between being a figure of fun, a shriveled windbag, and being a sinister threat to the integrity of anyone attracted to him. The eventual dismantling of the false community that had formed with Volpone as its "centre attractive" afforded Jonson the chance to address, in their own terms, those critics who claimed that "*we neuer punish vice in our* enterludes" (Epistle to *Volpone,* l. 116). Not that any true enemy of the stage would have been silenced by such a comic catastrophe, but it testifies to Jonson's passionate, even foolhardy, commitment to speaking out against those powerful conspiracies that threaten individual expression.

Chronology

1572	Ben Johnson born in London, probably on June 11, some time after his father's death.
(?)1574	His mother remarries a bricklayer.
1583–88	Attends Westminster School, studying under Master William Camden.
1588–96	Apprenticed to his stepfather; he also fights as a volunteer soldier in the wars in the Netherlands (exact dates unknown).
(?)1594	Marries.
1597	Acts in a strolling company and collaborates on *The Isle of Dogs* (now lost), for which he is imprisoned on charges of sedition.
1598	*The Case Is Altered* and *Every Man in His Humour* performed; he is imprisoned after killing an actor in a duel, but freed on pleading the right of clergy.
1599	*Every Man out of His Humour* performed.
1600	*Cynthia's Revels* performed.
1601	*Poetaster* performed.
1603	Son Benjamin dies. *Sejanus* performed, but hissed off the stage.
1605	Voluntarily goes to prison to join his collaborators Marston and Chapman (*Eastward Ho!*), who had been imprisoned on charges of mockery of the Scots.
1606	*Volpone* performed.
1609	*Epicoene* performed.
1610	*The Alchemist* performed.
1611	*Catiline* performed, unsuccessfully.
1612–13	Serves as tutor to the son of Sir Walter Raleigh on his French tour.
1614	*Bartholomew Fair* performed.

131

1616	Publishes a folio edition of his *Works; The Devil Is an Ass* performed; granted a government pension (which he never receives).
1618–19	Goes on walking tour of Scotland, visiting Drummond of Hawthornden along the way.
1619	Receives an Honorary M. A. from Oxford University.
1623	House destroyed by fire; some work in progress is lost.
1626	*The Staple of News* performed.
1628	Partially paralyzed by a stroke; appointed Chronologer of the City of London.
1629	*The New Inn* performed and hissed off the stage.
1632	*The Magnetic Lady* performed.
1633	*The Tale of a Tub* performed (probably written much earlier).
1637	Dies on August 6 and is buried in Westminster Abbey.

Contributors

HAROLD BLOOM, Sterling Professor of the Humanities at Yale University, is the author of *The Anxiety of Influence, Poetry and Repression,* and many other volumes of literary criticism. His forthcoming study, *Freud: Transference and Authority,* attempts a full-scale reading of all of Freud's major writings. A MacArthur Prize Fellow, he is general editor of five series of literary criticism published by Chelsea House. During 1987–88, he served as Charles Eliot Norton Professor of Poetry at Harvard University.

WILLIAM EMPSON was a distinguished poet and literary critic. His principle books include his *Collected Poems, Seven Types of Ambiguity, Some Versions of Pastoral,* and *The Structure of Complex Words.*

STEPHEN GREENBLATT, Professor of English at the University of California, Berkeley, is the author of *Sir Walter Raleigh: The Renaissance Man and His Role* and *Renaissance Self-Fashioning: From More to Shakespeare.*

LEO SALINGAR is a Fellow of Trinity College, Cambridge.

L. A. BEAURLINE is Professor of English at the University of Virginia. He has edited works by Ben Jonson, Beaumont and Fletcher, John Dryden, and Sir John Suckling, and is the author of *Jonson and Elizabethan Comedy: Essays in Dramatic Rhetoric.*

C. N. MANLOVE is Lecturer in English Literature at the University of Edinburgh. His works include *Literature and Reality 1600–1800* and *The Gap in Shakespeare.*

ANNE BARTON is Fellow of New College and University Lecturer in English, University of Oxford. She is the author of *Ben Jonson, Dramatist* and *Shakespeare and the Idea of the Play.*

WILLIAM W. E. SLIGHTS is a member of the English Department at the University of Saskatchewan.

133

Bibliography

Anderson, Mark. "Structure and Response in *Volpone.*" *Renaissance and Modern Studies* 19 (1975): 47–71.

Barish, Jonas A. *Ben Jonson and the Language of Prose Comedy.* Cambridge: Harvard University Press, 1960. Reprint. New York: Norton, 1970.

———. "The Double Plot in *Volpone.*" *Modern Philology* 51 (1953): 83–92.

Barton, Anne. *Ben Jonson, Dramatist.* Cambridge: Cambridge University Press, 1984.

Baum, Helena Watts. *The Satiric and the Didactic in Ben Jonson's Comedy.* Chapel Hill: University of North Carolina Press, 1947.

Beaurline, L. A. *Jonson and Elizabethan Comedy: Essays in Dramatic Rhetoric.* San Marino, Calif.: Huntington Library, 1978.

Broude, Ronald. "Volpone and the Triumph of Truth: Some Antecedents and Analogues of the Main Plot in *Volpone.*" *Studies in Philology* 77 (1980): 227–46.

Bryant, J. A., Jr. *The Compassionate Satirist: Ben Johson and His Imperfect World.* Athens: University of Georgia Press, 1972.

Creaser, John. "Volpone: The Mortifying of the Fox." *Essays in Criticism* 25 (1975): 329–56.

Dessen, Alan C. *Jonson's Moral Comedy.* Evanston, Ill.: Northwestern University Press, 1971.

Donaldson, Ian. "Volpone: Quick and Dead." *Essays in Criticism* 21 (1971): 121–34.

Duncan, Douglas. *Ben Jonson and the Lucianic Tradition.* Cambridge: Cambridge University Press, 1979.

Gibbons, Brian. *Jacobean City Comedy.* Cambridge: Harvard University Press, 1968.

Goldberg, S. L. "Folly into Crime: The Catastrophe of *Valpone.*" *Modern Language Quarterly* 20 (1959): 233–42.

Gossett, S. " 'Best Men Are Molded out of Faults': Marrying the Rapist in Jacobean Drama." *English Literary Renaissance* 14 (1984): 305–27.

Grene, Nicholas. *Shakespeare, Jonson, Molière: The Comic Contract.* London: Macmillan, 1980.

Hallett, Charles A. "Jonson's Celia: A Reinterpretation of *Volpone.*" *Studies in Philology* 68 (1971): 50–69.

———. "The Satanic Nature of *Volpone.*" *Philological Quarterly* 49 (1970): 41–55.

Hurd, Myles. "Between Crime and Punishment in Jonson's *Volpone.*" *College Literature* 10 (1983): 172–83.

Jackson, Gabriele Bernhard. *Vision and Judgment in Ben Jonson's Drama.* Yale Studies in English, vol. 166. New Haven: Yale University Press, 1968.

Kelly, Joseph John. "Ben Jonson's Politics." *Renaissance and Reformation* 7, no. 3 (August 1983): 192–215.

Kernan, Alvin. *The Cankered Muse: Satire of the English Renaissance.* New Haven: Yale University Press, 1959.

———. ed. *Two Renaissance Mythmakers: Christopher Marlowe and Ben Jonson.* Selected Papers from the English Institute, 1975–76, n.s. 1. Baltimore: The Johns Hopkins University Press, 1977.

Knights, L. C. *Drama and Society in the Age of Jonson.* London: Chatto & Windus, 1937. Reprint. New York: Norton, 1968.

Knoll, Robert. *Ben Jonson's Plays: An Introduction.* Lincoln: University of Nebraska Press, 1964.

Leggatt, Alexander. *Ben Jonson: His Vision and His Art.* London: Methuen, 1981.

———. "The Suicide of Volpone." *University of Toronto Quarterly* 39 (1969): 19–32.

Levin, Harry. Introduction to *Ben Jonson: Selected Works.* New York: Random House, 1938.

Levin, Lawrence L. "Justice and Society in *Sejanus* and *Volpone.*" *Discourse: A Review of the Liberal Arts,* no. 13 (1970): 319–24.

Miles, Rosalind. *Ben Jonson: His Life and Work.* London: Routledge & Kegan Paul, 1986.

Murray, Timothy. "From Foul Sheets to Legitimate Model: Antitheater, Text, Ben Jonson." *New Literary History* 14, no. 4 (Spring 1983): 641–64.

Nash, Ralph. "The Comic Intent of *Volpone.*" *Studies in Philology* 44 (1947): 26–40.

Orken, Martin R. "Languages of Deception in *Volpone.*" *Theoria* 59 (October 1982): 39–49.

Parfitt, George. *Ben Jonson: Public Poet and Private Man.* New York: Barnes & Noble, 1976.

Partridge, Edward B. *The Broken Compass: A Study of the Major Comedies of Ben Jonson.* New York: Columbia University Press, 1958.

Paster, Gail Kern. "Ben Jonson's Comedy of Limitation." *Studies in Philology* 72 (1975): 51–71.

———. *The Idea of the City in the Age of Shakespeare.* Athens: University of Georgia Press, 1985.

Pineas, Rainer. "The Morality Vice in *Volpone.*" *Discourse: A Review of the Liberal Arts,* no. 5 (1962): 451–59.

St. Pierre, Ronald. " 'So Rare a Musique out of Discordes': Chaos and Order in Ben Jonson's *Volpone.*" *Shoin Literary Review* 17 (1983): 1–14.

Simmons, Joseph L. "Volpone as Antinous: Jonson and 'Th' Overthrow of Stage-Playes.' " *The Modern Language Review* 70 (1975): 13–19.

Summers, Claude J., and Ted-Larry Pebworth, eds. *Ben Jonson.* Boston: Twayne, 1979.

———, eds. *Classic and Cavalier: Essays on Ben Jonson and the Sons of Ben.* Pittsburgh, Pa.: University of Pittsburgh Press, 1982.

Summers, Joseph H. *The Heirs of Donne and Jonson.* New York: Oxford University Press, 1970.

Swinburne, Charles Algernon. *A Study of Ben Jonson.* London: Chatto & Windus,

1889. Annotated reprint, edited by Howard B. Norland. Lincoln: University of Nebraska Press, 1969.

Thayer, C. G. *Ben Jonson: Studies in the Plays.* Norman: University of Oklahoma Press, 1963.

Weld, John. "Christian Comedy: *Volpone*." *Studies in Philology* 51 (1954): 172–93.

Acknowledgments

"*Volpone*" by William Empson from *The Hudson Review* 21, no. 4 (Winter 1968–69), © 1969 by *The Hudson Review*. Reprinted by permission.

"The False Ending in *Volpone*" by Stephen Greenblatt from *Journal of English and Germanic Philology* 75, nos. 1 & 2 (January–April 1976), © 1976 by the Board of Trustees of the University of Illinois. Reprinted by permission of the University of Illinois Press.

"Comic Form in Ben Jonson: Volpone and the Philosopher's Stone" by Leo Salingar from *English Drama: Forms and Development,* edited by Marie Axton and Raymond Williams, © 1977 by Cambridge University Press. Reprinted by permission of Cambridge University Press.

"Comic Language in *Volpone*" by L. A. Beaurline from *Jonson and Elizabethan Comedy: Essays in Dramatic Rhetoric* by L. A. Beaurline, © 1978 by the Henry E. Huntington Library and Art Gallery. Reprinted by permission.

"The Double View in *Volpone*" by C. N. Manlove from *Studies in English Literature 1500–1900* 19, no. 2 (Spring 1979), © 1979 by William Marsh Rice University. Reprinted by permission.

"*Volpone*" (originally entitled "Sejanus and Volpone") by Anne Barton from *Ben Jonson, Dramatist* by Anne Barton, © 1984 by Cambridge University Press. Reprinted by permission of the author and Cambridge University Press.

"The Play of Conspiracies in *Volpone*" by William W. E. Slights from *Texas Studies in Literature and Language* 27, no. 4 (Winter 1985), © 1985 by the University of Texas Press. Reprinted by permission of the University of Texas Press.

Index